The Queer Press Guide 2000

The Queer Press Guide 2000

Edited by

Paul Harris

Painted Leaf Press
New York City

www.paintedleaf.com

Published by Painted Leaf Press,
P.O. Box 2480 Times Square Station, NY NY 10108-2480.
Printed in Canada.

Cover design: Stuart Bagwell
Text design: Henry White

Library of Congress-in-Publication Data

Harris, Paul
            The queer press guide2000 / edited by Paul Harris.
                    p. cm.
            Includes index.
ISBN 1-891305-17-4
   1. Gay press--Directories. 2. Gay press--United States--Directories. I. Title

HQ76.9 .H37 1999
070.4'4930590664--dc21   99-04586

Contents

INTRODUCTION

When I was about sixteen or seventeen years of age and living in a small town in rural England an acquaintance let me look at his copy of "Gay News", the now defunct national newspaper that served the United Kingdom. I remember as if it was yesterday looking at it and reading stories and news items about people like myself. It was an important landmark moment in my sometimes painful and difficult journey towards accepting myself as a gay man.

That newspaper helped me to realize that there was a life out there for me, that I was not alone, indeed that there were others like me. At that stage I had already been published in a local newspaper and knew the excitement of seeing my byline on newsprint. Little did I know then that years later I would feel comfortable enough about myself to get published on a regular basis in gay newspapers and that I would be compiling a directory about these publications!

According to the most recent statistics, every ten days and 17 hours a gay or lesbian publication in the United States folds up. The good news is that every seven days and 14 hours another brave group of would-be publishers start another newspaper or magazine. As a result the gay and lesbian press has been one of the fastest growing areas of print media in the past twenty years. It has now reached the point that every major city in North America has at least one publication that seeks to serve its gay, lesbian, bisexual or transgender population, and of course many have considerably more.

This growth in the number of publications has been fueled by a number of factors - the growing number of businesses only too willing to spend part of their advertising budget in the gay marketplace, the growing numbers of men and women who feel comfortable enough about their sexuality to pick up the publications in public or semi-public places, and lastly, but far from least important, the growing numbers of gay and lesbian writers who are no longer afraid of self-identifying themselves by writing for these papers.

How things have changed! The late Jim Kepner who both founded and served as an officer of the ONE Institute and who was one of the most important figures in the early gay press in the Fifties wrote his columns in the magazine of the same name under a pseudonym until 1958. Today, however, in some cities politicians very often actively seek the endorsement of the local gay and lesbian publication in an attempt to appeal to an important segment of their electorate. Barbara Dozetos tells us in her essay that both Vermont's U.S. Senators and the congressman all subscribe to "Out In The Mountains".

As the gay and lesbian world has grown there has been a corresponding increase in the degree of specialization in the publications. Today we have publications targeted at gay black men and women, at the gay disabled, at those seeking to raise non-traditional families, at gay Christians, even gay airline travelers.

When, sometime in the latter part of the next century, a social historian sits down and tries to make sense of the gay and lesbian sexual revolution that has been taking place in North America since the end of the 1950's I cannot but think that the publishers and editors (many of whom would be making far better livings doing almost anything else!) will finally emerge as the heroes and heroines that they have been. To them I raise my metaphorical hat.

This book is an attempt to identify as many gay, lesbian, bisexual and transgender publications in North America as possible as well as listing some of the more important publications from around the rest of the world. It has been a difficult undertaking and one in which I have received considerable help from many sources whom I should like publicly to acknowledge. With just a few curmudgeonly exceptions the publishers and editors of our publications have been unfailingly helpful and courteous in completing a questionnaire and in answering further queries.

To more specific "Thank Yous".... There is a lesbian couple living in Omaha, Nebraska known throughout the gay activist world as "Fenceberry" - their AOL online name. Aleta Fenceroy and Jean Mayberry have devoted countless hours in acting as a clearing house for gay and lesbian news from all over the globe. As a result many of the rest of us, whether journalists or activists, have been able to contribute to the reporting, and comment upon events affecting our worldwide community. Early in my research they kindly passed on details of this project through their network. Long may they continue. Others, previously unknown to me, came out of the woodwork to help. Derek Barnett did his best to make sure that I knew about all the African American g/l/b/t publications, while Alex Galinda helped with Spain and Latin America. I received support throughout from many of my fellow gay and lesbian journalists and in particular Mike Frederickson up until the summer of 1999 the

Executive Director of the National Lesbian and Gay Journalists Association, an organization of which I am a proud member and would urge you to join. I should also like to acknowledge Charles Flowers of The Publishing Triangle for his support of the project. The Mulryan-Nash Advertising agency generously sent me their latest study of advertising trends in the g/l/b/t press.

In my personal circle I should like to mention my fellow members of "Q*ink," led by the indefatigible Scott Coatsworth. It is a weekly online discussion group of g/l/b/t writers and their friends who urged me onwards. Through "Q*ink" I met my good friend Hugh Coyle who nagged me into attending the "Out Write" Conference in Boston during the spring of 1999 where I had the good fortune to meet not only Barbara Dozetos, editor of "Out In The Mountains," who contributes the essay "Why The Gay Press Matters" but also Bill Sullivan, my publisher at Painted Leaf Press, who ironically lives only five blocks from my home in Hells Kitchen in Manhattan! I should also like to thank my fellow writer Shelly Roberts for taking the time to answer some questions about self-syndicating.

To them all I say a heartfelt "Thank You". Any errors that remain though are of course my own.....

Why The Gay Press Matters

by Barbara Dozetos
Editor of "Out In The Mountains"

The necessity of the queer press has been a popular topic for panels at writer's conferences and forums of late. Do we need media of our own? The answer is so often an emphatic "Yes!" that I'm left to wonder why the question keeps coming up. It's easy enough to agree that it needs to exist, but pinpointing the reasons and specifying the roles we expect the gay press to play requires more thought. Depending on our location and to varying degrees, queer folk rely heavily upon our press. Contrary to stereotypes, most of us do not reside in gay havens such as San Francisco, Key West, and Greenwich Village. As a matter of fact, some of us don't recognize the name of places like the Castro, Christopher Street, or West Hollywood as the meccas or icons they are supposed to be within queer culture. The queer press provides us with our definitions, our visibility, and our connections - both within the GLBT community and to the rest of the world.

How many of us, upon coming out, needed basic instruction in The Life? Didn't you long to sign up for a course called "Intro to Gay Life" or "Queer 101"? I know I did. But finding such a thing in Vermont, where there is a grand total of two gay bars in the entire state and no defined ghetto for hundreds of miles, was no simple task.

I found nothing on gay lifestyles or experiences in my local mainstream press. The decade-old books in the public library were a start, but I needed more. Then I stumbled across a newspaper called "Out In The Mountains." (Little did I know that I would end up editing it in the not-so-distant future.)

From the pages of that publication, I learned about the world I was finally allowing myself to join. Its very presence reassured me that there were indeed other GLBT folks in the area. Come to think of it, it was from the paper I learned about "GLBT" and "PWA" and "NGLTF" and all the rest of the alphabet soup that we bandy about.

The very first issue I read told me that one of my state legislators was very much an ally and another wasn't; for that matter, it taught me what an ally was in the first place. I found out about queer books and magazines, local groups and activities, where to meet other gay people and, of course, how to volunteer for the paper.

Picking up just one issue drew me into the queer community in my state and the rest of the world.

I believe connection is the press' most vital role. I know it's particularly true in our more rural communities. Without our publications, most non-urban queers would have few links to each other. A 16-year-old lesbian from the most rural part of our rural state recently wrote to tell me that without our paper, she would be "lost with no clue about gay people anywhere."

As we struggle to define or redefine ourselves, we need such points of reference. The queer media is vital in its provision of images with which we can identify. Without these, we are left to check off the long list of things we are not - and negative definition is hell on the self-image. Simply put, the queer press helps us to be....... well, queer. It also makes it easier for us to find one another. I'm not talking personal ads here, although they are certainly important to many people. I point, instead, to achievements such as the Gay and Lesbian Employees at Middlebury. This group formed as a direct result of an article one of my predecessors printed in our paper; that was no small feat on the campus of a very conservative college where very few people were comfortable being "out."

More recently, two students at the University of Vermont decided, as a class project, to investigate the possibility of a queer community center in our largest metropolitan area. A letter to the editor in our November 1998 issue asked for interested parties to join them. Over the next few months, they ran ads and updates in "Out In The Mountains." By March, they'd attracted so much interest they couldn't accommodate everyone at a dinner event during "Equality Begins At Home Week" and the next month hosted their first coffeehouse - with nearly 100 people in attendance.

The presence of a GLBT newspaper or magazine is also a sort of road sign. When we walk into a store or restaurant and see one of our publications amongst the others inside the door, we know that the establishment is at least welcoming, if not 100 per cent friendly or even "Family-owned." During my tenure as editor of "Out In The Mountains," I have received countless letters from people visiting or new to the area telling me about the joy, relief and comfort they felt seeing tangible evidence that there is a queer presence in the area. Almost as gratifying are letters from across the spectrum of the straight community, telling me that they have learned something valuable from our pages or trying to perhaps explain the straight world to us. Even the nastiest comments help us to know our enemies, allow us to practice our arguments, and often prove our points for us.

Some of the mainstream media outlets do make an effort to cover us and our stories, but where do you think they get their ideas and information? I know for a fact that a reporter for one Vermont daily reads "Out In The Mountains" faithfully. I know not just because she reports on the same stories, but because she sub-scribes to the paper and calls me for contacts and follow-up. Our newspapers and magazines not only tell us about each other, but give our allies and the rest of the world reliable sources of informa-tion. The queer press teaches the straight world about us.

Our publications are an important resource for politicians and others who should serve the community. By reading what we write for and about ourselves, they gain valuable insight into our situa-tions. Every member (all three) of Vermont's congressional delega-tion subscribes to "Out In The Mountains", and a large stack of each issue is delivered directly to our State House. They do pay attention. (Of course, our opposition and detractors watch us just as closely. We take the bad with the good.)

In my mind, the ultimate proof of the necessity of the queer press is in its continued existence. I know we are needed because when the fifth of the month rolls around and someone's paper hasn't arrived, I get a call. I know because people stop me on the street and in the laundromat and at community functions to tell me so - to thank us for the work we do and tell us how important the paper is to them. I know because many dedicated volunteers have made sure that "Out In The Mountains" has existed for more than 13 years - and I know that we are not the only paper with stories like this to tell.

The National Lesbian and Gay Journalists Association

Who We Are?

Since its founding in 1990, NLGJA has grown to a 1,350-member, 23-chapter organization in the United States and Canada with an affiliate in Germany. The issues of same-sex marriage, gay families, parenting and adoption, gays in the military, sex education in the schools, civil liberties, gay-related ballot initiatives, gay bashing and anti-gay violence are commanding media attention with regularity. NLGJA has had a positive effect on responsible gay coverage, but we still have work to do.

Members and participants of NLGJA come from some of the most respected print, broadcast and online newsrooms and from a broad cross-section of gay and lesbian media. Members are in newsrooms such as The New York Times, Windy City Times, The Boston Globe, OUT Magazine, Associated Press, FOX, Philadelphia Gay News, Chicago Tribune, Los Angeles Times, The Philadelphia Inquirer, ABC, NBC, CBS, CNN, Gay News Network and PBS.

NLGJA Mission

NLGJA works within the news industry to foster fair and accurate coverage of lesbian and gay issues and opposes newsroom bias against gays and lesbians and all other minorities. NLGJA provides networking opportunities for lesbian and gay journalists, media professionals and communication/journalism students on local, national and international levels.

Are We Political?

NLGJA keeps its members informed of legislative issues that impact gays and lesbians through our website, e-mail and our newsletter. We do not, however, lend our name to, nor participate as a group in political action events or organizations.

NLGJA Goals

•Enhance the professionalism, skills and career opportunities for gay and lesbian journalists

•Strengthen the identity, respect and status of gays and lesbians in the newsroom and throughout the practice of journalism

•Advocate for the highest journalistic and ethical standards in the coverage of gay and lesbian issues

•Collaborate with other professional journalist associations and promote the principles of inclusion and diversity within our ranks

•Provide mentoring and leadership to future journalists

NLGJA Programs

•NLGJA's Stylebook Addenda on Gay and Lesbian Terminology, written by journalists for journalists, provides guidance for the language used in articles about lesbians and gays.

•The "Get the Word Out" program advocates for the fair and accurate coverage of lesbian and gay issues and trains representatives of gay and lesbian and AIDS organizations on effectively working with the news media.

•The NLGJA Domestic Partner Benefits: A Trend Toward Fairness handbook is a step-by-step guide that is a valuable resource to everyone from lesbian and gay journalists to employees at Fortune 500 companies. NLGJA has assisted in securing DP benefits in more than 78 newsrooms.

•The NLGJA Website (www.nlgja.org) offers information on services and special events and is a forum for discussion of issues concerning lesbian and gay journalists.

•NLGJA members and NewsWatch track inferior and inaccurate coverage of the gay and other minority communities. In addition, they take a stand on these issues using in-depth articles on a website and in a quarterly NewsWatch magazine.

•The Media Diversity Circle, a local organizing effort, builds bridges between NLGJA and other journalism and communications groups committed to diversity.

•NLGJA Campus Conferences provide educational tools to future journalists - gay and non-gay to cope with the complex social issues around sexual orientation as reflected in the news media.

•Print, Broadcast and Online juried cash awards encourage excellence in the coverage of issues concerning the lesbian and gay community.

NLGJA Member Benefits

As an NLGJA member you will be part of a network of hundreds of professionals who share your commitment to newsroom fairness and accuracy. In addition, we provide you with:

"Alternatives," NLGJA's quarterly newsletter provides in-depth coverage of the state of the gay story and workplace issues such as domestic partner benefits, and updates the reader on Association activities at the national and chapter level.

Networking opportunities with media professionals who have been there, done that. Whether attending our receptions, conventions, chapter panels and special events, you will have access to contacts like nowhere else.

Access from remote and rural regions of the country and world. Our website and national office can open doors to help support you, even if you have no local contact with other lesbian and gay journalists. And, our caucuses to address specific interests, such as Small Market, Public Radio, New Media, Gay and Lesbian Press, and Women connect throughout the year via e-mail.

Discounted admission to the Annual NLGJA Convention that attracts more than 500 attendees interested in the state of the gay story and skills building. Past headliners have included CBS's Dan Rather and Lesley Stahl, Texas columnist Molly Ivins, NBC's Tom Brokaw, print and broadcast journalist Linda Ellerbee, and openly gay journalists Achy Obejas of the Chicago Tribune and CNN's Edward Alwood.

Connection to one of NLGJA's 23 chapters which work at the local level to bring gay and lesbian news-coverage issues to the forefront by hosting panel discussions with local newsroom decision-makers, pitching gay and lesbian-related news stories and speaking out when the local media distort images of the gay and lesbian community.

Entry into the Convention Career Expo where newsrooms come to you looking for openly gay and lesbian reporters, producers, promotion directors, copy editors, and other media professionals.

Representation of your issues at the Council of Presidents of Journalism Organizations, the Board of the Radio-Television News Directors Association and the Diversity Committee of the Newspaper Association of America. NLGJA leaders also attend professional meetings such as the Asian American Journalists Association, National Association of Hispanic Journalists, National Association of Black Journalists and Native American Journalists Association conventions, as well as The Freedom Forum, and The Maynard Institute for Journalism Education.

NLGJA members are bringing their knowledge of covering the gay and lesbian community to students across the nation by:

•Speaking in classrooms at campuses such as San Francisco State University, Emory University, Indiana University and George Mason University.

•Mentoring young gay and lesbian journalists on how to come out in the newsroom and how to be good journalists.

•Bringing students to the annual convention to work on the Student Website, Video and Radio Projects. Scholarships are provided from contributions by NLGJA members and supporters.

NLGJA took bold stands against inaccurate and distorted news coverage of the gay and lesbian community. Some recent accomplishments include:

•The New York chapter of NLGJA featured openly-gay (Casper, WY) Star-Tribune political reporter Jason Marsden and local editors and producers on the "Does Someone Have to Die for the Press to Cover Bias Attacks?" panel examining the coverage of hate crimes. The National Association of Hispanic Journalists co-sponsored this event.
•NLGJA spoke out against the sweeps month trend on local broadcast affiliates of airing lurid images of men having sex in public bathrooms. NLGJA's opinion was voiced on CNN's Reliable Sources, in The Village Voice, and in Howard Kurtz's media column in The Washington Post.
•When Time magazine released its 75th-anniversary issue, ignoring the gay and lesbian civil rights movement and the AIDS epidemic, NLGJA was on the case. After discussions with editors, the hardcover book version includes an early look at society's reaction to the AIDS crisis and Tony Kushner's Angels In America contribution to theater.

NLGJA publications bring our voice to newsroom decision-makers. NLGJA research and information helped to create change in the following recent areas:

•Domestic partner benefits were expanded to more than 10 newsrooms in 1998, bringing fair workplace benefits to gay and lesbian employees in more than 115 newsrooms across the nation. Recent success stories include The Washington Post, CNET online news, Sacramento Bee, New Times, Inc. alternative newsweeklies, and The Chicago Reader.

•The Stylebook Addenda on Gay/ Lesbian Terminology is affecting the language used in articles about the gay and lesbian community in the mainstream press. Outdated words are replaced with more sensitive and accurate terminology.

•Alternatives updates members and the industry on the work and mission of NLGJA, bringing gay and lesbian coverage issues to the forefront.

National Staff

Acting Executive Director: Pamela Strother   nlgjapam@aol.com
Program Director: Craig Seymour nlgjacraig@aol.com
Executive Assistant: David Douberly   nlgja@aol.com

How to contact the National Lesbian and Gay Journalists Association:

Write to them at:
National Lesbian & Gay Journalists Association
2120 L Street, NW
Suite 840
Washington, DC 20037
Call or fax them at: 202.588.9888 tel 202.588.1818 fax
E-mail them at: nlgja@aol.com
or visit their website at www.nlgja.org

The Publishing Triangle:
The Association of Lesbians and Gay Men in Publishing

Founded in 1988, The Publishing Triangle began as a professional networking group that soon expanded to producing national programs that promote and celebrate lesbian and gay literature. As we enter our 11th year, the Triangle has accomplished two major goals: the opening of a new office at the prestigious Mercantile Library in January 1999 and the launch of our website (www.publishingtriangle.org) in June 1999.

On the local level, the Triangle works to create support and a sense of community for lesbian and gay people in the publishing industry by offering forums of discussion, as well as networking and social opportunities, for our members. Each year, we produce four to six events focused on some aspect of publishing, such as "Publishing 101: Everything You Need to Know About Getting Into Print," or "Funny Money: How to Write and Sell Humor." Members of the Triangle receive discounts on the entrance fee to these events, which are open to the general public as well.

On the national level, the Triangle has four major activities:
1) National Lesbian and Gay Book Month, 2) The Triangle Awards,
3) BookAIDS, and 4) the Publishing Triangle News.

NATIONAL LESBIAN AND GAY BOOK MONTH

Begun in 1991, National Lesbian and Gay Book Month (NLGBM) occurs each June, in conjunction with Gay Pride activities around the nation. In 1999, as part of NLGBM, the Triangle announced a list of The 100 Best Lesbian and Gay Novels. The list was selected by a jury of fourteen writers and critics, including Dorothy Allison, David Bergman, Michael Bronski, Christopher Bram, Samuel R. Delany, Lillian Faderman, Anthony Heilbut, M.E. Kerr, Jenifer Levin, John Loughery, Jaime Manrique, Mariana Romo-Carmona, Sarah Schulman, and Barbara Smith. The list was displayed on a poster that was included in a promotional kit that was sent free to the over 700 bookstores and libraries across the country that participate in NLGBM.

THE TRIANGLE AWARDS

The Triangle Awards are presented each spring by the Publishing Triangle, in association with The Robert Chesley Foundation, and include six awards: The Bill Whitehead Award for Lifetime Achievement, The Ferro-Grumley Awards for Lesbian and Gay Fiction, The Randy Shilts-Judy Grahn Awards for Lesbian and Gay Nonfiction, and The Robert Chesley Award for Lesbian and Gay Playwriting.

The Bill Whitehead Award for Lifetime Achievement recognizes a body of work with significant lesbian and gay content. It is awarded in memory of longtime Dutton Editor-in-Chief Bill Whitehead, who worked with such writers as Doris Grumbach, Anne Rice, and Edmund White. The Bill Whitehead Award for Lifetime Achievement is made possible by bequests of George Stambolian and Allan Barnett.

Only members of the Publishing Triangle may nominate candidates for the Whitehead Award. In addition, Triangle members elect a panel of six judges, serving staggered three-year terms; two new judges, one female, one male, are selected each year. Recipients must be living and may not have received the award previously. In even-numbered years, the award goes to a woman; in odd-numbered years, to a man. Each award carries a $3,000 honorarium.

Previous Winners of the Bill Whitehead Award for Lifetime Achievement include John Rechy (1999), M.E. Kerr (1998), Armistead Maupin (1997), Joan Nestle (1996), Jonathan Ned Katz (1995), Judy Grahn (1994), Samuel Delany (1993), Audre Lorde (1992), James Purdy (1991), Adrienne Rich (1990), and Edmund White (1989).

Founded by the estates of Robert Ferro and Michael Grumley, The Ferro-Grumley Awards recognize excellence and experiment in literary fiction. Books of short stories are eligible, while books of poetry are not. Only books published in 1999 are eligible for the awards to be announced in March, 2000.

All current members of the Publishing Triangle may nominate books for free. All others must enclose a check for $25 per title nominated. (There is no limit on the number of titles nominated.) New members may nominate for free if nominations are accompanied by a check for $30, representing annual membership dues. Nominations from publishers should be accompanied by four copies of the nominated books (or bound galleys if books are not available), in addition to a check for $25 per title. All checks should be made

payable to: The Publishing Triangle.
    DEADLINE: October 1, 1999

Please mail ballots, checks, and books to: The Publishing Triangle, 17 East 47th Street, Third Floor, New York, NY 10017. If you have additional questions, please contact us at (212) 588-8867 or email us at awards@publishingtriangle.org

Previous Winners of the Ferro-Grumley Awards for Lesbian and Gay Fiction:

1999	Patricia Powell (The Pagoda)
	Michael Cunningham (The Hours)
1998	Elana Dykewoman (Beyond the Pale)
	Colm Toibin (The Story of the Night)
1997	Persimmon Blackbridge (Sunnybrook)
	Andrew Holleran (The Beauty of Men)
1996	Sarah Schulman (Rat Bohemia)
	Felice Picano (Like People in History)
1995	Heather Lewis (House Rules)
	Mark Merlis (American Studies)
1994	Jeanette Winterson (Written on the Body)
	John Berendt (Midnight in the Garden of Good and Evil)
1993	Dorothy Allison (Bastard Out of Carolina)
	Randall Kenan (Let the Dead Bury Their Dead)
1992	Blanche McCrary Boyd (The Revolution of Little Girls)
	Melvin Dixon (Vanishing Rooms)
1991	Cherry Muhanji (Her)
	Allen Barnett (The Body and Its Dangers)
1990	Ruthann Robson (Eye of the Hurricane)
	Dennis Cooper (Closer)

Established in 1997, the Randy Shilts-Judy Grahn Awards for Nonfiction are meant to honor books with significant influence upon lesbians and gay men. "Lesbian nonfiction" is defined as nonfiction affecting lesbian lives. The book may be by a lesbian, for example, or about a lesbian or lesbian culture, or both. The same is true of gay male nonfiction. Please feel free to be creative with your nominations. Only books published in 1999 are eligible for the awards to be announced in March, 2000. The nominating procedure is the same as for the fiction awards (see above).

Previous Winners of the Shilts-Grahn Awards for Lesbian and Gay Nonfiction:

1999   Judith Haberstam (Female Masculinity)
       John Loughery (The Other Side of Silence)
1998   Margot Peters (May Sarton)
       David Sedaris (Naked)
1997   Bernadette Brooten (Love Between Women)
       Anthony Heilbut (Thomas Mann)

Established to honor the memory of playwright Robert Chesley, the Robert Chelsey Award for Lesbian and Gay Playwriting may recognize a body of work or an emerging talent. The award alternates between a woman and a man, and each recipient recieves a honorarium of $1,000. For more information, please contact Victor Bumbalo at 828 North Laurel Avenue, Los Angeles, CA 90046.
Previous winners of the Robert Chesley Award:
1999: Madeleine Olnek
1998: Chay Yew
1997: Paula Vogel
1996: Robert Patrick, Susan Miller
1995: Victor Lodato
1994: Lisa Kron, Doric Wilson

BOOKAIDS

Now in its fourth year, BookAIDS was established by the Publishing Triangle to provide free books to men, women, and children living with HIV and AIDS. Under the guidance of Stanley Ely, longtime member of the Triangle, publishers donate 5,000 books a month to thirteen AIDS service organizations across the country. Publishers contributing on a semiannual basis include Penguin Putnam, Doubleday, Ballantine, Bantam, Avon, and Dell (as well as BDD Audio). In addition, Turtle Point Press, Kitchen Table Press and Alyson Books of Los Angeles make occasional contributions. Children's books from D.C. Comics and Simon & Schuster are also distributed at AIDS Project Los Angeles.
The recipients include AIDS Project Los Angeles, Los Angeles Gay and Lesbian Center, San Francisco AIDS Foundation, the AIDS Resource Center in Dallas, Boston's Fenway Community Health Center, Little Rock's Ryan White Center, the Howard Brown Health Center in Chicago, Washington's Whitman-Walker Clinic, Denver's Colorado AIDS Project, the Positive PWA Coalition in Provincetown, Gay Men's Health Crisis and Callen-Lorde Community Health Center in New York City, and Aid for AIDS of Nevada in Las Vegas.   Based

on the success of the program in America, BookAIDS Canada began in the spring of 1999 in Toronto, with guidance from the U.S. project.

THE PUBLISHING TRIANGLE NEWS

Published six times a year, the PT News keeps members in touch with industry trends and issues. Members can announce the publication of their upcoming workds, publicize calls for submissions, read profiles of small presses and booksellers, catch up on Triangle events, and raise questions about lesbian and gay publishing.

MEMBERSHIP

Membership is open to anyone interested in the growth of lesbian and gay writers, literature, and publishers. Members come from all walks of life: book and magazine writers, editors, agents, marketing, sub-rights, publicity and sales people, booksellers, designers, librarians, and general book lovers. Annual dues are $30 and are tax-deductible as a business expense. The benefits to membership are: discounts to events, nominating and voting privileges for the Triangle Awards, a subscription to the Publishing Triangle News, access to the mailing lists of NLGBM, and the knowledge that you are supporting the Triangle in its efforts to promote lesbian and gay literature.

To join the Triangle, please provide the following information in a letter: Name, Address, and Phone/Fax/Email. From time to time, the Triangle shares its mailing list with other groups we believe offer something of interest to our members. Please indicate in your letter if you would prefer not to be included in such mailings. Enclose a check for $30 (made payable to The Publishing Triangle) and send to Membership, The Publishing Triangle, 17 East 47th Street, Third Floor, New York, NY 10017.

If you have additional questions about the Triangle and its programs, please call (212) 588-8867 or email us at chair@publishing-triangle.org.

Q*ink!
Lesbigaytrans Writers & Friends Community

A free service for LBGT writers and friends. We have:

*Two weekly chats (one on AOL, one off) where you can make friends, talk shop or whatever's on your mind regarding any and all aspects of being a writer and being lesbigay. Established authors, editors and publishers are also invited to attend.

Q*ink! AOL meets Thursday nights at 10 PM ET on AOL at key-word WCCHAT, in the writer's den room.

Q*ink! Lesbian Writer's Chat meets on Wednesday at 11 PM ET at http://www.gay.com/pages/qink.html.

*A web site (http://www.mongooseontheloose.com/qink/index.html) that has bunches of Calls for Submissions, pages for current members (both free basic pages and longer Storyteller pages which have complete short stories and chapters of work), and lots of other helpful informtion.

*A free biweekly newsletter listing Calls for Submissions, member announcements, and bookstore and other events.

Q*ink! is the place to keep in touch with the LBGT writing community and a great place to network. To become a member, email Pherrin26@aol.com

How To Self-Syndicate

It is hard to make a living writing for the queer press. An article can be about an important subject, dear to your heart, you can research your material thoroughly, get it taken by a small newspaper or magazine, but when the modest check arrives, it hardly seems worth the effort. One way to increase your earnings and to increase the readership for your work is to "self-syndicate".

Syndication means that your article gets published more than once, although in wholly different geographical markets. Many writers fall at the first fence. They think it is beyond them. The reality is that it is relatively easy. Indeed since the onset of the Internet, it is easier today than at any time in the history of publishing! In addition with the increase in the number of publications out there looking for copy and the fact that most publications employ relatively few writers many of them rely upon material that they buy from freelancers. That freelancer could be you!

The same rules apply as if you were thinking of submitting an article to a single publication. Ask yourself, does your article and its subject matter belong in a particular publication? If you have written an article about a situation that is of no interest to anyone outside of a certain city, plainly readers in other cities will have no interest in reading about it. If however, you are reporting upon, or commenting about something or someone who has national significance you are writing something that has the makings of a syndicated article.

If you are not offering your article to a national magazine you can offer it literally all over the country to the multitude of queer publications . Once a publication in a certain part of the country or city agrees terms to buy it though you cannot sell it to anyone else in that particular geographical market. For example, if "Windy City Times" agree to buy an article of mine I cannot turn around and sell it to "Outlines!" or "Gay Chicago Magazine". An editor or publisher will go berserk if he or she sees an article that his or her publication has purchased in his competition's pages - and rightly so. This is another instance of why good record-keeping is important.

Some people who write syndicated articles make an agreement with a publication to provide it with a whole series of articles over a period of time, while other writers seek to syndicate their work as and when they have something worthwhile to sell. The advantage of having an ongoing agreement with a publisher or editor is that you know you have pre-sold at least some of your future writing. The disadvantage is that you have agreed to produce articles at a rate of one a week, or one a month on a particular subject whether you have something to say that week or month or not. While many writers respond well to the discipline of having to write an article to fulfill a contractual obligation, with others the thinness of some of their pieces can be obvious.

If you are seeking an ongoing agreement to syndicate with a particular publication you will have to negotiate precisely about what you are going to write every month so that your work does not overlap with that of another writer who is either on-staff or freelancing for them. This too has the advantage of forcing you to focus on a particular area but the disadvantage of restricting you perhaps from writing about more interesting subjects that come across your desk.

If you are planning on writing an article that you are going to syndicate nationally, or even internationally, it is important to see that the copy you write reflects the diversity of possible readers. If I am writing an article about mental health in the lesbian and gay community I should not speak to psychiatrists and psychologists who all come from Miami. Look for people across the country to interview if you plan on selling your piece nationwide. Once the article is written and you are happy with it, you are ready to send it out.

This is where the changes in technology make life much easier for us. With email you need only send the article out once with a multiple mailing. Place the email addresses in a way in which the mail will be copied to them. On AOL it is very easy. Put you own address in the "mailing to" box then put the email addresses of all the publications that you are going to query inside brackets in the cc box. In this way you will not be sending out your entire mailing list to everyone and you won't be wasting space when your article arrives on the editor's screen.

Under subject write "Submission to Editor" followed by the title of the piece and your name if there is space. Before pasting your article into the text space you should write a cover letter. It should look something like this:

Dear Editor,
Please find following my article about................. If you are interested in purchasing it please contact me ASAP on (999) 555 1234 or by emailing me at (your email address) to discuss the fee.

Previous recently syndicated articles have discussed the following subjects. If you would like to see any of these articles please email or call me.

Best wishes,

Your name
++

This is simple and to the point. If you have a photographic image that you can send electronically at a later time at the end of the article say "Photo(s) Available" along with the word count and "Copyright with your name and the year".

Once the publications start getting back to you and you agree terms to allow them to publish your article keep a clear record of whom you have sold to, precisely who you discussed it with, and the price agreed. In agreeing terms find out whether they are paying you immediately or upon publication. In addition find out whether they require an invoice. Thankfully, most publications nowadays, in my experience, don't. If you are to be paid on publication make a note of the day in your appointment book so that on that date you can send out an invoice. Very often invoices can be sent by email or faxed, again saving time and cost.

After a while you will find out which papers and magazines overlap with others and will know automatically whether you are free to sell the article to a publication or not. While speaking with an editor or publisher use the opportunity to find out what other types of article he or she is looking to purchase. This is valuable information. Perhaps he has just lost his movie critic. Is that a job for you?

While the majority of people who syndicate their writings charge for their work some do not. They syndicate their writings as a way of getting across their particular message, or of using the article as a means of advertising their professional services or writings that appear in book form and from which they make the bulk of their income. While this can be annoying to the rest of us who seek to make our livings from writing for queer publications it is simply a matter of fact and there is little that we can do about it.

One of the more successful self-syndicators is Shelly Roberts. She was good enough to answer some questions based upon her experience:

1. *What made you decide to start self-syndicating?*

There was absolutely no other choice. I wished to write once and get paid often. I also wished to write exclusively for/to the glbt market.There was/is no established syndicate either of significant quality, or at all worth considering.

2. How do YOU decide how much to charge a particular publication?

It has always been a "what the traffic will bear" situation. Most glbt publications are outgrowth newsletters, or lifelong under-financed dreams. I also chose to let my voice be more important than my wallet at the outset. So I offered my column widely, and free to non-profits. I usually asked for whatever the standard column fee was. Most papers that were going to pay paid honestly and fairly. Those that chose to be difficult often made writers wait 120 - 180 days from publication. Usually it was because they were cash flow tight, and didn't see that writers were providing the saleable product.

3. Do you self-syndicate primarily for the immediate financial rewards (don't start giggling now!) or to publicize your other published writings?

See above answer. It always struck me that the purpose of the columns for me was three fold. 1) to deliver my message in a more palatable (in my case humorous most of the time) way than I had been reading when I started, which was 1990. 2) To publicize my humor and style in support of my books and other activities. And 3) as a way to gain access...by access, I mean both to the newsmakers who welcomed me more freely from familiarity with my name, if not necessarily my work, and to the non-famous glbt members, for whom my work is mostly written, and from whom my work, information, and insight comes.

Now, after nearly ten years at it, I would like to be paid better, more often and more consistently, so I am considering spending more time monitoring the publication incidence, but probably, I won't. It is nearly impossible to monitor, not economically efficient, and, with the internet now playing such a wide distribution role, hard to anticipate doing effectively. Fortunately, mostly I have another means of support that doesn't require a huge amount of my time, and pays very well. My national advertising writing credentials stand me in good stead for affording my real work. And those pieces I financially monitor to the penny.

4. How have you built up your network including the foreign papers that you sell to?

I started with one newsletter to re-exercise my column-writing muscles. (I'd done a national monthly computer humor column in the '80's.) Many people think that they can capture the universe in 750-850 words, but it is a real discipline. My advertising training, which forced me to deliver crisp, concise, readable message in specifically limited space really forms the base for being effective, and in establishing beginning - middle - end communication. My message has always been glbt positive, and that has been a major factor in my columns acceptance.

From the first group newsletter, I was approached by the statewide paper, and agreed to stay exclusive with them for six months. After that I agreed to stay exclusive in the state with them, in their genre, for another year. (Magazine formats were not included in that exclusivity agreement.) But I was then free to solicit other papers outside their venue.

During that period, I collected enough printed clips to send out solicitation letters to glbt papers. I would do it every quarter, and send out letters to as many papers as I could find the addresses for. Initially I did it snail mail, and saw the cost as an investment in myself. First one, then a couple more, then a dozen came in. About that time email and the internet was taking hold, and I began solicitation over the net to the glbt pubs. Then papers around the country began to contact me to ask to carry the column. Since I no longer have to pay the long distance fax charges, I can now distribute the column easily to anyone with an email address.

Additionally, I subscribe to a couple of glbt news groups with wide distribution, and have a list of papers I am carried in only occasionally. My column, which is usually written bi-monthly, goes out to all those potential publishers with a onetime reprint right included in the copyright notice, permission for non-profits to reprint without cost, and an email address to contact me for commercial reprinting. For the most part, people have been honest and sent checks. Where they haven't, I can only hope that what they printed reached some 18 year old on the verge of suicide and persuaded her or him that s/he isn't alone, that s/he isn't some kind of freak of nature, and that tomorrow just might be a bit better, even fun in the living for. That's the real payback anyway. I think even if I were attempting to live off the proceeds of the column, it would still be the real payback. I'd just be living a bit better.

Occasionally I get pseudo-nostalgic for the monetary remunerations that might come if I were syndicated as widely in mainstream papers. But I sigh and go on.

5. *How do you deal with papers that are tardy payers?*

I just try to keep reminding them that they owe me honest money for honest work. No point in threatening them with pulling the column. That would defeat my purpose. I know one journalist who was so adamant about being paid that, for papers which are almost always on the raw edge of survival, she was quickly a liability, and they just dropped her, and never paid. I find that I've made far more $10/$20/$45 dollars at a time by being accessible. But as I said in the previous answer, I have another source of income.

6. *What simple advice would you offer to a fellow journalist seeking to start self-syndicating?*

Make sure that your really have something to say. Nobody wants to hire a parrot, even a clever one. Make sure that you know who you are talking to in your writing. Carve yourself a niche. When I started the field was nearly clear. I could count the columnists on the fingers of one hand and a couple of thumbs. Now everybody R one. So you need a point of difference. That's what makes you viable and saleable. People need to say to your editor, "I love the paper, and I always turn to the Shelly Roberts (Insert your name here) section first. I just love her. Thanks for carrying her column." When you have one paper where people are saying that, then take four of your best samples and offer it to a set of other papers. If you've done the first things I suggest, and there's room at the in (sic) you'll pick up more papers. It is a book-keeping nightmare to self-syndicate, and a tedious burden to keep track. But until someone decides to create an effective syndicating company, you have no other choice. Besides, when that company does decide to do that, and I know of three which have it in the talking stage as I write this, they will want to pick up proven writers who can produce revenue, so you might as well start collecting your samples now. But most of all, if you really want to do it, be persistent, and be patient. Oh, yes, and if no one is congratulating you on what you've just written, for god's sake, stop and go do something else. Not everyone can. Not everyone should. If some of us make it look easy, then it's just because we've been doing it for a very long time.

7. *Have you ever used a syndicating business? What were the results?*

I tried a couple of times, but found the operations way too small and inefficient. So far no one's been able to crack the glbt newspaper/ magazine world for syndication. Probably because it's too full of independents, under-capitalizeds, gone-belly-up-ers, and devoted hobbyists to make doing it right worthwhile. I hope that changes. I hope they call me immediately.

Shelly Roberts is an internationally syndicated humor columnist whose "Roberts' Rules" column appears in over 100 gay and/or lesbian publications and on the internet. Shelly is a speaker, MC, and semi-professional Grand Marshall.

Her best-selling books include the Roberts' Rules of Lesbian Living, of Lesbian Break-ups and of Lesbian Dating, The Dyke Detector, Hey Mom, Guess What! And Roberts' Rules of Daily Living 1999 calendar.

Shelly is producing The Rainbow Celebration Concert, a non-political, three-day, nationwide GLBT concert, October, 13-15th, 2000, "to celebrate what we did, in concert."

An alternative to self-syndicating is to have someone else do it for you. The earnings are very much less but you don't have the hassle of contacting the publications or collecting your earnings. Effectively they buy the article from you.

The two of whom we are aware are

Full Court Press who syndicate horoscopes to the g/l/b/t press. They can be reached at P.O. Box 50536, Nashville TN 37205 and

Q Syndicate which is the largest provider of content to the gay and lesbian press, offering publishers more than a dozen columns and features to choose from: an editorial cartoon; a crossword puzzle; a word search puzzle; a cartoon strip; a political insider column; a progressive lesbian political commentary column; a conservative Republican political commentary column; a travel column; a history column; a Hollywood insider column; a horoscope; capsule movie reviews; and capsule book reviews. To find out more about Q Syndicate, visit their Web site, www.qsyndicate.com, call 1-888-383-7911 or write to Rawley Grau, Editor in Chief, Q Syndicate at QSEditor@aol.com

National

ABLE TOGETHER

Regularity of Publication: Quarterly
Circulation: Approximately 200, w/ a Data Base of 1800 former sub-
scribers, interested parties, potential subscribers, to whom we send
promotional materials, sample issues, etc.
Audited: No
U.S. Voice Mail: (415) 522-9091   U.K. Voice Mail: 01452 832782
Fax Number: (415) 864-6817
E-mail address: General: ABLTOGETHR@aol.com
Editor: Gayedit@aol.com
website address: http://www.well.com/user/blaine/abletog.html
EDITOR: (415) 864-6817
Average length of feature: 2,000-3,000 words
We do not pay contributors.
How do you prefer your stories to be filed? E-mail/files
How do you prefer to be contacted? E-mail
Special needs of your publication: Humor; Arts Reviews; Celebrity profiles.
What is the best advice for someone contemplating writing for your publication? Our
focus is on first-person accounts by disabled gay men, although we
will consider submissions by women or nondisabled men.

The Advocate

Liberation Publications Inc
6922 Hollywood Blvd, Suite 1000, Los Angeles CA 90028
Regularity of Publication: Biweekly except for monthly issues in
January and August
Phone Number: 323 871 1225   Fax Number: 323 467 6805
E-mail address: info@advocate.com   newsroom@advocate.com
website address: www.advocate.com

Publisher: Joe Landry
Editor in Chief: Bruce C. Steele
Managing Editor: Michael W. Elkins
Senior News editor: John Gallagher
Advertising Managers: Greg Brossia, Erica Springer

Allboy Magazine

COLOR INK CORP. 736 NE 72ND ST, Miami, Fl. 33138
phone: 305-754-2090   fax: 305-754-BOYZ (2699)
Email: webmaster@allboymag.com

Alternative Family Magazine

P.O. Box 7179, Van Nuys, CA 91409
Regularity of Publication: Bi-monthly from January
Circulation: 20,000   Audited: No
Phone Number: (818) 909-0314   Fax Number: (818) 909-3792
E-mail address: altfammag@aol.com
website address: http://www.altfammag.com
Publisher: Paul Obis (708) 386-4770
Editor in Chief   Kelly Taylor (818) 909-0314
altfammag@aol.com
Managing Editor: John Quinlan (608) 251-2452
altfammag2@aol.com
Advertising Manager: Kelly Taylor (818) 909-0314
Average length of feature: 2,000 words
Minimum rate paid per word: 10 cents
Minimum rate paid for photos: $25
How do you prefer your stories to be filed? electronically
How do you prefer to be contacted? via email
Special needs of your publication: Articles, essays, cartoons,
interviews and news (both national and local) pertaining to the interests of GLBT parents and their children. Also interested in general
parenting and family health articles without the heterosexual bias.
What is the best advice for someone contemplating writing for your publication? Be
well aware that our audience includes younger children who read the
magazine. Do not include any sexually explicit items or use any type
of foul language. Also, look for photo-driven articles - our readers
enjoy seeing other families. Seek out the "heros" and local parent-

ing groups in your area that are doing something positive for our families. We're always looking for teen (the children of GLBT parents) issues relating to their families and peer situations.

American Bear / American Grizzly

Amabear Publishing, Inc., PO Box 7083, Louisville KY 40257-7083
Regularity of Publication: American Bear is Bi-monthly,
American Grizzly is Quarterly
Phone Number: 502-894-8573
E-mail address: amabear@iglou.com
website address: www.amabear.com
Editor: Tim Martin
Advertising Manager: Sheryl Soderberg
What is the best advice for someone contemplating writing for your publication?
Contact us for information.

ANGLES

The Policy Journal of the Institute for Gay and Lesbian Strategic Studies

Circulation: 2,000   Audited: No
Regularity of Publication: Quarterly
Ph#: (413) 577-0145
FAX: (413) 545-2921
Email: badgett@iglss.org
www.iglss.org
Editor: Lee Badgett
Average Length: 3,000 words
email best way to contact
Policy Analysis is our focus
If you need any further information please do not hesitate to contact us. You can check out Angles on our Website: http://www.iglss.org

Anything That Moves bisexual magazine

The Magazine for the Uncompromising Bisexual

261 Market St., #496, San Francisco, CA 94114-1600
Three times/year

Circulation: Approximately 12,500   Audited: no
Phone Number: (415) 626-5069
E-mail address: info@anythingthatmoves.com
website address: www.anythingthatmoves.com
Managing Editor: Linda Howard
(editrix@anythingthatmoves.com)
News Editor: Charles Anders
Reviews Editor: Kevin McCulloch
Poetry Editor: Jenny Bitner
Advertising Manager: Rav Usi
Average length of feature:Maximum of 2,500; preferred 1,500-2,000
Minimum rate paid per word: N/A (Two contributor's copies)
Minimum rate paid for photos: N/A (Two contributor's copies)
How do you prefer your stories to be filed?
Email to submit@anythingthatmoves.com
How do you prefer to be contacted?
Email to info@anythingthatmoves.com or via phone
Special needs of your publication that freelance writers might be able to fulfill: Part of Anything That Moves' mission is to provide as diverse view of the bisexual, transsexual, and gender fluid community as possible; we especially welcome submissions on international issues and from demographic areas we have not heard from. We also welcome well-researched news articles on issues and events within the queer community.
What is the best advice for someone contemplating writing for your publication?
Please read and follow our subscription guidelines, and feel free to ask for clarification or inquire about story ideas via submit@anythingthatmoves.com.

Bent Magazine

PO Box 3701, Beverley Hills, CA 90212
Phone Number: 310 278 2331   Fax: 310 278 2331
E-mail: info@bentmagazine.com
Publisher: publisher@bentmagazine.com
Editor: R. Alexander Jaime   editor@bentmagazine.com

BiNet News

BiNet USA, 4201 Wilson Blvd #110-311, Arlington, VA 22203-1859
Regularity of Publication: Quarterly
Audited: No
Phone Number: (202)986-7186
E-mail address: newsletter@binetusa.org
website address: http://www.binNetUSA.org/
Editor: Wendy Curry
Average length of feature: 750 words
Minimum rate paid per word: $0
Minimum rate paid for photos: $0
How do you prefer your stories to be filed? electronically, emailed to
newsletter address
How do you prefer to be contacted? email: wendyc@BINetUSA.org
Special needs of your publication: Bisexual focussed news, views, essays,
art, photos, reviews. Interest in Bisexual slants on "Gay/Straight
issues", such as: hate crimes, domestic violence, discrimination,
coming out, family life...
What is the best advice for someone contemplating writing for your publication? Join
BiNetUSA! Its not required, but it enables you to easily get the
newsletter.

Black Sheets

PO Box 31155-QPG, San Francisco, CA 94131-0155
Regularity of Publication: Two to three times yearly.
Circulation: 7,000   Audited: No
Phone Number: (415) 431-0171   Fax Number: (415) 431-0172
E-mail address: QPG@blackbooks.com   BlackB@queernet.org
website address: http://www.blackbooks.com
Publisher: Black Books
Editor: Bill Brent
Advertising Manager: Tracey Darling
Average length of feature: up to 3000 words
Minimum rate paid per word: n/a; $10 to $25 per article
Minimum rate paid for photos: $10/photo
How do you prefer your stories to be filed?   email
How do you prefer to be contacted?   email
Special needs of your publication: Contact us for current guidelines and

themes of upcoming issues.
What is the best advice for someone contemplating writing for your publication?
Read the magazine BEFORE submitting anything to us. We are a
humorous magazine about sex and popular culture. Emphasis is on
SEX.We are polymorphously perverse and omnisexual.

Bulk Male

AfterImage Studios
3020 Bridgeway Suite 184, Sausalito, CA 94965
Phone/Fax: (415) 339-8816
Bimonthly
Bulk Male magazine is the premier publication for large men and
their counterparts.
Submitting artwork of literature: Our guidelines are simple: Your story or
artwork has to do with large men and their admirers. If it's a story, it
must be typed, and limited to 8 pages double spaced. If you are
doing it on a computer, send it to us on disk with hard copy. We can
use either Mac or PC formats saved as 'Simple text', 'Word', 'ASCII'
or 'Text' only. If it's art work, we can reproduce any medium.

Centaur Magazine

"In Celebration of the Senior Male"

PO Box 1326, Desert Hot Springs,CA 92240
Phone Number: 760 251 2091
E-mail: ctar@earthlink.net

Circles

1705 Fourteenth Street, Suite 326, Boulder, Colorado 80302
Regularity of Publication: Quarterly
Circulation: Circulation 8000+   Audited: No
Phone Number(s): (303) 245 8815 (business)
888 633 0055 (subscriptions)   Fax Number: (303) 245 8816
E-mail address: circles@circlesmagazine.com
website address: http://www.circlesmagazine.com
Publisher and Editor: Kit McChesney
Advertising Manager: Kit McChesney (303 245 8815)

Average length of feature: words 1500-3000
Minimum rate paid per word: Arranged by negotiated NWU contract
Minimum rate paid for photos: Arranged by negotiated NWU contract
How do you prefer your stories to be filed? Query first
How do you prefer to be contacted? by letter or email
Special needs of your publication: Lesbian issues
What is the best advice for someone contemplating writing for your publication? All interested writers must submit a detailed query first; most of our accepted submissions are from writers who are already engaged in investigative or research projects, rather than fulfillments of commissioned pieces.

Circuit Noize

East Coast Office, PO Box 22656, Fort Lauderdale, FL 33335
West Coast office,
11288 Centura Boulevard #700, Studio City, CA 91604
Phone(s):   west - 954 764 8210 east 818 769 9390
Fax(s):   west - 954 764 6392 east 818 769 5482
E-mail: info@circuitnoize.com
website: www.circuitnoize.com
Publisher: Stephen Ceplenski
Editor in Chief: Steve Kammon
Advertising Director: Gary Steinberg
Advertising Sales: Wade Rchey 323 871 0166
wadxe@cicuitnoize.com

Clikque Magazine

931 Monroe Dr., Ste. 102-279, Atlanta, GA 30308
Regularity of Publication: Monthly
Circulation: 25,000 copies
Phone Numbers: 404-486-9655 or 888-504-5703
Fax Number: 404-235-0613
E-mail address: clikquem@aol.com
Publisher and Editor: Dwight Powell
Co-Editor: Lewis Nicholson
Average length of feature: At least 450 words
How do you prefer your stories to be filed? We prefer for them to be sent as text file via email.

How do you prefer to be contacted? We would like to be contact via phone or email.

Special needs of your publication: We need more Lesbian news and views.

What is the best advice for someone contemplating writing for your publication? Our advice for someone contemplating writing for us would be that their work will be looked at as an art work, and won't be overlooked. We will also offer our opinion on the article and its contents.

Curve Magazine

One Haight Street, Suite B, San Francisco, CA 94102
Regularity of publication: Bimonthly
Circulation: 69,000
Phone 415 863 6538   Fax   415 863 1609
E-mail address Curvemag@aol.com Curvead@aol.com
Writecurve@aol.com
Currently construcing website. Have address on Planet out Keyword: Curve
www.curvemag.com
Publisher/Editor in Chief: Frances Stevens
Managing/News editor: Gregtchen Lee
Advertising manager: Frances Stevens 415 863 6538
Average length of feature 1200-1800
Minimum rate per word 10c
Minimum for photos $25.00
The best way to contact publication: Fax or phone
The best way to file: e-mail
Special Interests: Exclusively lesbian coverage; National News, Celebrity profiles, Lesbian news and views. Curve is the nation's best selling lesbian magazine, focusing on lesbian culture, entertainment, politics and fashion

Cybersocket, The Gay Net Directory & Cybersocket Web Magazine

Cybersocket LLC, 7510 Sunset Blvd., Suite1203, Los Angeles, CA 90046
Regularity of Publication: Cybersocket Directory - Annually each Fall
                    Cybersocket Magazine - Quarterly
Circulation: 30,000 each annual edition of Directory
30,000 each issue of Magazine   Audited: No
Phone Number:213-484-6261   Fax Number: 213-484-6262

E-mail address: info@cybersocket.com
website address: www.cybersocket.com
Publisher: Cybersocket LLC 213-484-6261
Managing Editor: Tim Lutz
Advertising Manager: Morgan Sommer
Average length of feature: 800 words
Minimum rate paid per word: 15 cents
Minimum rate paid for photos: $50-100
How do you prefer your stories to be filed? Email
How do you prefer to be contacted? Phone or Email
Special needs of your publication: All aspects of Gay and Lesbian culture are to be included and discussed. But particular emphasis is upon using web refernces in features or in-depth website reviews, tech info, or interviews with leaders in this medium.
What is the best advice for someone contemplating writing for your publication? All interested parties should call or email for a media kit and copies of our publications and be Web savvy.

Dignity USA Journal

1500 Massachusetts Avenue, Suite 11, Washington, DC 20005
Regularity of Publication: Quarterly
Circulation: 3,500   Audited: No
Phone Number: 202-861-0017   Fax Number: 202-429-9808
E-mail address: dignity@aol.com
website address: www.dignityusa.org
Editor: David Floss, 219-484-6492,
e-mail: DAFloss@aol.com
Advertising Manager: David Floss, 219-484-6492,
e-mail: DAFloss@aol.com
Average length of feature: 1,500 words
Minimum rate paid per word: 0
Minimum rate paid for photos: 0
How do you prefer your stories to be filed? E-mail
How do you prefer to be contacted? Contact editor directly regarding sub-missions or advertising.
Special needs of your publication: Anything and everything of particular interest to GLBT Catholics, their families and friends.

EDGE MAGAZINE

6434 Santa Monica Blvd, Hollywood, CA 90038
Phone: 323 962 6994
E-mail: edgemag@earthlink.net
Publisher: Dennis Colby

Brenda Loew's EIDOS Magazine:
Sexual Freedom andErotic Entertainment for Consenting Adults

P.O. Box 96, Boston, MA 02137-0096
Regularity of Publication: Quarterly
Circulation: 12,000   Audited: No
Phone Number: 617-262-0096   Fax Number: 617-364-0096
E-mail address: eidos@eidos.org
website address: www.eidos.org
Publisher/Editor: Brenda Loew
Advertising: Brenda Loew
Average length of feature: 500-2500 words
Minimum rate paid per word: Contributor copy & byline
Minimum rate paid for photos: Contributor copy & byline
How do you prefer your stories to be filed? On a floppy disk formatted for
Macintosh. Do not email us manuscripts, poetry, art or photos.
How do you prefer to be contacted? In writing with an SASE include
an 18+ age statement.
Special needs of your publication: EIDOS is a forum for the discussion and
examination of mutually respectful, consensual depictions and repre-
sentations of erotic and sexual orientations, preferences and
lifestyles. We are especially seeking original erotic photography and
artwork for publication.
What is the best advice for someone contemplating writing for your publication?
EIDOS is an upscale, unique independent periodical that advocates
and defends freedom of personal erotic and sexual expression as a
human, constitutional and civil right. We highly suggest perusing our
current issue and even a back issue or two before submitting material.

The Family Tree

P.O.Box 34337, San Diego, CA 92163
Regularity of Publication: quarterly
Circulation: 4,000   Audited: No
Phone Number: (619) 296-0199
Fax Number: (619) 296-0699
E-mail address: program@familypride.com
website address: www.familypride.org
Publisher: Suzette Southfox, Program Director
Editor: Dale Rosenberg
Average length of feature: depends
Minimum rate paid per word: n/a
Minimum rate paid for photos: n/a
How do you prefer your stories to be filed? electronically
How do you prefer to be contacted? email
Special needs of your publication: LGBT parents, parenting, families

Foot Buddies Magazine

Stone House Publishing,P.O. Box 13490, Chicago, IL 60613-3490
Regularity of Publication: Quarterly
Circulation: 250 Audited: No
Phone Number(s): 773-665-8174/312-458-0824
E-mail address: bfb@ix.netcom.com
website address http://www.footbuddies.com
Publisher: Gene Janowski
What is the best advice for someone contemplating writing for your publication?
Have a gay male foot fetish.

Gay Black Female Magazine "GBF"

6312 Hollywood Blvd #23, Hollywood, CA 90028
Regularity of Publication: Monthly
Circulation: 160,000   Audited: No
Phone Number: 323 376 2157
Fax Number: 213 381 1305
E-mail address: GBF@pacbell.net
website address: www.gayblackfemale

Publisher/Editor: Stephanie Wynne 323 376 2157
sdw@gayblackfemale.com
Managing Editor: Ta'shia Asanti
Average length of feature: 2,500 words
Minimum rate paid per word: 0
Minimum rate paid for photos: 0
How do you prefer your stories to be filed? e-mail, disk
How do you prefer to be contacted? e-mail disk
Special needs of your publication: Short stories, poetry
What is the best advice for someone contemplating writing for your publication?
Have something to say

GBM

2215-R Market Street #148, San Francisco, CA 94114-1653
Regularity of Publication: Bimonthly
Circulation: 20,000   Audited: Yes
Phone Number: (415) 552-1506   Fax Number: (415) 552-3244
E-mail address: gbm@brushcreek.com
website address: www.brushcreek.com
Publisher: Bear Dog Hoffman (ext.104)
Editor: Graylin Thornton (ext.122)
Managing Editor: Peter Millar (ext.110)
Advertising Manager: Willis Johnson (ext.106)
Average length of feature:1000 words
Minimum rate paid per word: negotiated
Minimum rate paid for photos: negotiated
How do you prefer your stories to be filed? electronically
How do you prefer to be contacted? e-mail
What is the best advice for someone contemplating writing for your publication?
Contact us first

GCN (Gay Community News)

29 Stanhope St., Boston, MA 02116
Regularity of Publication: quarterly
Circulation: 4,000   Audited: No
Phone Number: 617 262-6969   Fax Number: 617 267-0852
E-mail address: merlien@bsef.terranet.com
website address: www.bsef.org

Publisher: Bromfield St. Educational Foundation (ext. 2)
Editor: Marla Erlien (ext. 1)
Advertising Manager: Cynthia Peters (ext. 2)
Average length of feature: 1500-2500 words
Minimum rate paid for photos: $15.00
How do you prefer your stories to be filed? on disk or email
How do you prefer to be contacted? mail or email
What is the best advice for someone contemplating writing for your publication?
Just send the manuscript

Gay Airline and Travel Club Newsletter

P.O. Box 69A04, West Hollywood, CA 90069
Email: gayboylaca@writeme.com
Phone: 323 650 5112
Publisher: Louis Wendruck

Gay Parent magazine

P.O. Box 750852, Forest Hills, New York 11375-0852
Regularity of Publication: Bi-monthly
Circulation: 10,000 + (also published entirely on the internet)
Audited: No
Phone Number: (718) 793-6641   Fax Number: call for fax number
E-mail address: gayparentmag@banet.net
website address: http://www.gayparentmag.com
Publisher/Editor: Angeline Acain
Average length of feature: 1000 words
Minimum rate paid per word: 10 cents
Minimum rate paid for photos: negotiable
How do you prefer your stories to be filed? e-mail
How do you prefer to be contacted? Phone or e-mail
Special needs of your publication: All articles pertaining to the theme of lesbian and gay parenting will be considered. Humor pieces and celebrity profiles are always a plus. I'm interested in local or national news especially if it is about laws concerning adoption, foster care or gay parenting.
What is the best advice for someone contemplating writing for your publication? Keep

the word count to approximately 1000 words and your article must be on the topic of lesbian and gay parenting.

Gay Theological Journal

c/o Mentor Press, 8571-B Sudley Road, Manassas, VA 20110
Regularity of Publication 3 times a year
Circulation: 1,500   Audited: No
Phone Number: 703-330-5600   Fax Number: 703-330-5357
E-mail address: gaytheojrnl@pubpartners.com
website address: http://www.pubpartners.com/gaytheojrnl.html
Publisher and Editor: Bruce Joffe
Advertising Manager: Russ Warren
Average length of feature: 1,500 words
How do you prefer your stories to be filed? Query first; then submitted on disk using Microsoft Word 5.1 for Macintosh
How do you prefer to be contacted? E-mail, fax or letter
Special needs of your publication: Gay Theological Journal deals ONLY with religious, spiritual and biblical matters of concern to GLBT people of faith.
What is the best advice for someone contemplating writing for your publication? Study several issues first before contacting us!

GAY TRUCKERS CLASSIFIEDS

P.O. Box 1102, Brenham, Texas 77834
Regularity of Publication: Monthly
Circulation: 2000+   Audited: No
Phone Number: 409-836-0735   Fax Number: 409-830-8718
E-mail address: leducq2@worldnet.att.net
website address: www.gaytrucker.com
Publisher   Tim Page
Editor: Tim Page
Managing Editor: Scott Langley
Advertising Manager: Scott Langley/Tim Page
Average length of feature: 2/3/4 pages
Minimum rate paid per word: free for subscribers
Minimum rate paid for photos: free for subscribers
How do you prefer to be contacted? mail
Special needs of your publication: Total Trucker road sex. Ads, personals etc.

40

What is the best advice for someone contemplating writing for your publication?
Things you have always wanted to know about road sex with
Truckers and Admirers. Truckers looking for Admirers/looking for
Truckers. Lots of HOT Trucker Photos.

Genre

7080 Hollywood Blvd. #1104, Hollywood, CA   90028
Regularity of Publication: Monthly
Circulation:approximately 45,000 paid & unpaid   Audited: Yes
Phone Number: (323) 467-8300   Fax Number: (323) 467-8365
E-mail address:genre@aol.com
website address: www.genremagazine.com
Publisher: Richard Settles (ext. 17)
Editor: Morris Weissinger (ext. 19)
Managing Editor: J.P. Pfeffer (ext. 12)
Creative Director: Ric Ferrari (ext. 20)
Senior Editor: Seth Flicker
Advertising Manager: Richard Settles (ext. 17)
Average length of feature: 5000 words
Minimum rate paid per word: $500/feature
Minimum rate paid for photos: $100
How do you prefer your stories to be filed? Mac Disc
How do you prefer to be contacted? phone & e-mail queries

Girlfriends Magazine

3415 Cesar Chavez, Suite 101, San Francisco, CA 94110
Regularity of Publication: Monthly
Circulation: 75,000
Phone Number: (415) 648-9464   Fax Number: (415) 648-4705
Customer service: 1.800.GRL.FRND
E-mail address: staff@gfriends.com
website address: www.gfriends.com
Publisher: Erin Findlay
Editor in Chief: Heather Findlay
editorial@gfriends.com
Managing Editor: Kathleen Hildenbrand
Features Editor: Kathleen Hildenbrand
Arts Editor: Sarah Friesema

News Editor: Kathleen Hildenbrand
Advertising Manager: Catherine Draper
Average length of feature: 3000 words
Minimum rate paid per word: negotiable
Minimum rate paid for photos: $30/photo; up to $300 for pictorials
How do you prefer your stories to be filed? Hardcopy or email. If email, must
be ascii text or formatted for Microsoft Word 6, Macintosh.
How do you prefer to be contacted? Snail mail
Special needs of your publication: Lesbian news, views and events.
What is the best advice for someone contemplating writing for your publication?
Read our magazine, then request our submission guidelines. Be
sure to include an SASE. We are not currently accepting poetry, and
strongly discourage unsolicited fiction submissions for fiction.
Freelancers, please query first.

Harrington Gay Men's Fiction Quarterly

c/o Brian Bouldrey, 2215R Market Street, Suite 101
San Francisco, CA 94114
Tel: (415) 431 2574   Fax: (415) 431 2574
Regularity of Publication: Quarterly
Publisher: Bill Cohen (ext. 329)
Editor   Brian Bouldrey Tel: (415) 431 2574
Advertising Manager: Jackie Blakeslee (ext. 346)
Average length of feature: 5-15 pages
What is the best advice for someone contemplating writing for your publication?
Harrington Gay Men's Fiction Quarterly is being published under the
Harrington Park Press Southern Tier Editions imprint. The Harrington
Park Press Southern Tier Editions are committed to presenting a
vision of gay men's lives - in fiction and in popular accessible nonfic-
tion - in all its richness and diversity. Cutting-edge fiction by some of
America's most talented gay writers, reportage from the frontiers of
contemporary queer culture, and true accounts of love, sex, and
desire in the real world - Southern Tier Editions will focus on the
lifestyles of gay men, rough edges and all, in a publishing program
that promises to be controversial, enlightening, and entertaining.

Harrington Lesbian Fiction Quarterly

c/o Judith P. Stelboum, 360 East 72nd Steet, #B1502,

42

New York, NY 10021
Tel: (212) 988-7266   Fax: (212) 517-6727
Regularity of Publication: Quarterly
Publisher: Bill Cohen (ext. 329)
Editor: Judith P. Stelboum   Tel: (212) 988-7266
Advertising Manager: Jackie Blakeslee (ext. 346)
Average length of feature: 1 - 25 pages
How do you prefer your stories to be filed? By hard copy and disk by mail
How do you prefer to be contacted? Mail, E-Mail or by phone
Special needs of your publication: Short stories, poetry, novel excerpts, memoirs and essays should be focused on aspects of Lesbian writing or culture. Drawings and photography will also be considered.
What is the best advice for someone contemplating writing for your publication?
"Send the best you have" There are no restrictions on genre or content. Harrington Lesbian Fiction Quarterly will be published under the Harrington Park Press Alice Street Editions imprint. The Harrington Park Press Alice Street Editions will provide a voice for lesbian fiction, essay, memoir, and popular nonfiction. Alice Street seeks to capture the vitality and splendor of the lesbian erotic experience in all of its diversity. This imprint welcomes the opportunity to present controversial views, explore multicultural venues, encourage debate, and inspire creativity within the lesbian sensibility: Lesbian fantasy, humor, erotica, remembrance, will come to life in the pages of Alice Street Editions.

The Harvard Gay & Lesbian Review

PO Box 180300, Boston, MA 02118
Regularity of Publication: Quarterly
Circulation: 10,000   Audited: No
Phone Number: 617-421-0082   Fax Number: Call first.
E-mail address: HGLR@aol.com
website address: www. HGLR.com
Editor and publisher: Richard Schneider, Jr. 617-421-0082
Assistant Editor: Drew Rapp 617-421-0082
Advertising Manager: David Yegerlehner 212-879-7439
Average length of feature: 3000 words
Minimum rate paid per word: We do not pay for articles at this time.
Minimum rate paid for photos: We do not pay for photos at this time.
How do you prefer your stories to be filed? Submissions in hard copy.
How do you prefer to be contacted? E-mail or regular mail.

Special needs of your publication: Essays that deal broadly with gay and lesbian history, politics, and culture. We also publish book reviews as well as movie and theatre reviews. More articles from women and minorities would be welcome.
Note: We do not publish short fiction.
What is the best advice for someone contemplating writing for your publication? Ask yourself the question, Will this article still be worth reading a few years from now?

HERO Magazine

[note: the word HERO is ALL CAPS]
8581 Santa Monica Blvd. PMB 430, West Hollywood, CA 90069
Regularity of Publication: Bi-monthly
Circulation: 60,000   Audited: Yes
Phone Number: 310-360-8022
E-mail address: info@heromag.com
website address: http://www.heromag.com
Publisher: Sam Francis
Editorial Director: Paul Horne phorne@heromag.com
Technology Editor   Eric Mueller
Arts Editor: Jeffrey L. Newman
Advertising Manager: Sam Francis
Average length of feature: 2-3,000 words
Minimum rate paid per word: 20 cents
Minimum rate paid for photos: $25
How do you prefer your stories to be filed? email
How do you prefer to be contacted? Regular mail. We do NOT under any circumstances accept inquiries or sample writing via email or fax.
Special needs of your publication: HERO stories are positive, inspirational, and well-balanced. We cover romance and relationships, families, youth and over-40, entertainment, technology, pop culture, and humor. We are not interested in erotic fiction, circuit parties, or porn stars.
What is the best advice for someone contemplating writing for your publication? Read the magazine first! If you haven't read HERO, we can usually tell by the first paragraph of your cover letter. Only amateur writers submit to magazines they've never read, and we get too many submissions to waste time on those. Also, we expect our writers to have email.

44

IN THE FAMILY

The Magazine for Lesbians, Gays, Bisexuals and Their Relations

PO Box 5387, Takoma Park, MD 20913
Regularity of Publication: Quarterly
Circulation: 7,000   Audited: NO
Phone Number: 301-270-4771
E-mail address: LMarkowitz@aol.com
website address: www.inthefamily.com
Publisher/Editor: Laura Markowitz 301-270-4771 (ext. 2)
Arts Editor: Michael Leclair 301-270-4771 (ext. 3)
Advertising Manager: Neala Harris 301-270-4771 (ext. 4)
Average length of feature: 4,000 words
Minimum rate paid per word: varies
Minimum rate paid for photos: varies
How do you prefer your stories to be filed?
How do you prefer to be contacted? Mail
Special needs of your publication: Book reviews, clinical case studies
What is the best advice for someone contemplating writing for your publication?
Read a copy of it to get a good idea of what we publish

IN UNIFORM The Magazine

PO Box 3226, Portland, OR 97208-3226
Regularity of Publication: Quarterly
Circulation: 5,000   Audited: No
Phone Number: 503-228-6935   Fax Number: 503-228-3190
E-mail address: UniformMag@aol.com
website address: www.teleport.com/~uniform
Publisher: Andy Mangels
Editor: Andy Mangels
Advertising Manager: Andy Mangels or Don Hood
Average length of feature: 2,000-4,000 words
Minimum rate paid per word: negotiated
Minimum rate paid for photos: negotiated
How do you prefer your stories to be filed? Electronically
How do you prefer to be contacted? Phone or email
Special needs of your publication: Articles solely of interest to
Uniform/Military/Police/ Sports fetishists and enthusiasts.
What is the best advice for someone contemplating writing for your publication?

Know something about the fetish market, and query us before writing.

The International Gay & Lesbian Review

Walter L. Williams, Editor,
International Gay and Lesbian Review,Anthropology Department,
University of Southern California Los Angeles, CA 90089-0032
Publisher: The One Institute Press
Editor: Walter L. Williams
walterlw@usc.edu or by phone at (213) 740-1911.

Please provide complete bibliographic information for the item being reviewed as requested. Complete information makes it far easier for individuals reading the review to then locate the book themselves. Providing publisher information is vital, since many non-metropolitan areas will not have specialized bookstores that stock these titles. These readers will need the publisher information in order to purchase the book directly.

Begin your Review with an abstract explaining the book's subject matter and the author's major conclusions, since unpublished works, and even numerous published books, are unavailable (especially to unemployed people and to many people in developing nations). Note there is a specifically labeled ABSTRACT field in the SUBMIT REVIEW submission form. Reviewers should not assume that readers will be reading, or even have access to, the book under review.

Following the ABSTRACT, the reviewer should also give an evaluation of the book, explaining where the book makes contributions to the field, mentioning the book's strengths, and assessing it weaknesses. If applicable, point out any special, noteworthy or unusual information, illustrations, or other distinguishing content that would be of significant interest.

Reviewers are encouraged to give constructive critiques and substantive, yet concise, comments that will be of help to readers, researchers, and authors alike. International Gay & Lesbian Review is not an unmoderated discussion forum. All submissions will be reviewed and evaluated by the editors for inclusion. Authors agree that in submitting their review, they consent to editorial changes/modifications that do not change the meaning of their text. International Gay & Lesbian Review is not able to return submissions.

The submission of a review to International Gay & Lesbian Review implies that the author certifies that neither the article nor any of its parts is copyrighted or currently under review for any refereed journal or conference proceedings. If the article, any portion of it, or any other version of it, has appeared, or is scheduled to appear in another publication of any kind, the details of such publication must be made known to the editors at the time of submission.

The readers of International Gay & Lesbian Review come from many nations, many disciplines, and from outside academia; therefore, reviewers should write in jargon-free, clear language that is accessible to a larger audience. Racist, sexist, heterosexist or other discriminatory writing will not be published, but the editors encourage expression of a wide spectrum of lesbian and gay ideas, reflecting the diversity of homoerotically inclined people in different nations, classes, ethnicities, ages, and genders. When writing your review, please keep in mind the diversity of the audience of International Gay & Lesbian Review

Instinct Magazine

11638 Ventura Blvd., Studio City, CA 91604-2613
Regularity of Publication: BiMonthly
Phone Number: 818-505-9205   Fax Number: 818-505-9875
E-mail address: mail@instinctmag.com
website address: www.instinctmag.com
Publisher: JR Pratts
Editor in Chief: Gabriel JP Goldberg
Advertising Manager: JR Pratts
Average length of feature: Feature: 1,500-3,000 words;
Smaller articles: 800-950 words
Minimum rate paid per word: about 20 cents
Minimum rate paid for photos: $50.00
How do you prefer your stories to be filed? I just like 'em sent to me on paper.
How do you prefer to be contacted? Email or regular mail is fine. Or you can call. That's OK too.
Special needs of your publication: Anything that's funny, wacky, a bit left of center, maybe even a bit sick and wrong (we'll probably like it then). We're a bit politically INcorrect, for a gay magazine anyway, so our goal is to offend at least one or two people every issue (if we get more, that's even better).
What is the best advice for someone contemplating writing for your publication? Have a sense of humor. If you can make me laugh, hard, you're pretty much in.

James White Review

PO Box 73910, Washington, DC 20056-3910
Regularity of Publication: Quarterly
Circulation: 7000   Audited: No
Phone Number: 202-462-7924   Fax Number: 202-462-5264
E-mail address: JWRMerla@aol.com
website address: www.lambdalit.org
Publisher: Jim Marks 202-462-7924
LBBROJimM@aol.com
Editor: Patrick Merla
Managing Editor: Jim Marks 202-462-7924
Average length of feature: 5000 words
Minimum rate paid per word: The James White Review pays up to $150 per writing
Minimum rate paid for photos: Approximately $50 for photos/artwork
All fees are at the discretion of the editor.
How do you prefer your stories to be filed? MS Word, on disk.
How do you prefer to be contacted? Mail.
Special needs of your publication: The James White Review is a gay men's literary journal. Priorities go to fiction, poetry, literary non-fiction and critical essays. Most of the work is solicited by the editor, but we are interested in submissions.
What is the best advice for someone contemplating writing for your publication?
First, read the magazine to make sure your writing is in the spirit of the publication. The James White Review is dedicated to presenting the finest new writing by emerging and established writers alike. Work needs to be truly distinctive—innovative, deeply moving, highly original—to appear in the JWR.

Joey Magazine

11901 Santa Monica Blvd. Suite 598, Los Angeles, CA 90025
Publication frequency: Quarterly
Circulation: 20,000.   Audited: No
Phone number: 888-550-5639   Fax number: 310-388-1139
E-mail: joeymagzne@aol.com or joeymag@joeymag.com
Website: www.joeymag.com
Publisher: Jerry Dunn
jerry@joeymag.com 888-550-5639 ext 0

Editor: Leif Strickland
leif@joeymag.com 888-550-5639 ext 3
Email is the fastest and easiest way to contact us. We check it several
times a day.
Direct all advertising inquiries to the publisher. The print magazine is
distributed nationally, but we also offer local businesses various
advertising opportunities in our comprehensive CityGuide on our
website.
Average length of feature: Varies. We are interested in everything
from 300 word essays to 2000 word feature articles.
Special needs: Joey Magazine is aimed at gay and bisexual guys under
the age of 25, with the majority of our coverage on the teen segment. So we're looking for material that would be helpful, useful, or
entertaining to this audience. The tone should be appropriate to the
subject matter, but we're generally looking for writing that is fun,
fresh, and upbeat. Acceptible topics would include dating, friend-
ships, family, fashion, trends, fads, coming out, school, and so forth.
We also publish profiles of young guys who have an interesting story
to tell about their lives.

Prospective writers should mail, fax, or email the editor two or three
writing samples, along with a 100 to 200 word query detailing the
story he or she would like to write for Joey Magazine.

Minimum rates: Rates for photos and articles are negotiable. Some
are flat rates, others are per-word. We arrive at a price depending
on the length, quality, and amount of work involved. In the past, we
have paid as little as $25 for a short essay that we published on our
website, up to as much as $800 for a thoroughly researched 2000
word feature article.

The Journal of Bisexuality

c/o Fritz Klein, MD,4545 Park Blvd. #207, San Diego, CA 92116
Tel: (619) 542-0088   Fax: (619) 542-0006
Regularity of Publication: Quarterly
Circulation: Due to begin publication in 2000. Audited: No
Publisher: Bill Cohen
Editor: Fritz Klein, MD Tel: (619) 542?0088
Advertising Manager: Jackie Blakeslee
Average length of feature: 5 - 15 pages
Special needs of your publication: All issues concerning bisexuality
What is the best advice for someone contemplating writing for your publication? Get

in touch with the editor.

Journal of Gay & Lesbian Psychotherapy

c/o Jack Drescher, MD,420 West 23rd Street, 7D New York, NY 10011
Prefers all correspondence to be sent via the mail.
Regularity of Publication: Quarterly
Circulation: 750   Audited: No
Publisher: Bill Cohen
Editor-in-Chief: Jack Drescher, MD
Editors: Ann D'Ercole, Ph.D,
                         Joseph P. Merlino, Md.,
                         Christina Sekaer, MD, Ph.D
Advertising Manager: Jackie Blakeslee
Average length of feature: 5 - 15 pages
How do you prefer your stories to be filed? This is a scholarly, peer
reviewed journal.
How do you prefer to be contacted? Articles should be mailed to:
JOURNAL OF GAY & LESBIAN PSYCHOTHERAPY
4514 Chester Avenue, Philadelphia, Pennsylvania 19143-3707.
Telephone Number: (215) 222-2800
Special needs of your publication: none
What is the best advice for someone contemplating writing for your publication?
To read a few issues.

Journal of Gay & Lesbian Social Services

c/o James J. Kelly, PhD, MSW Dean,School of Health and Human
Services, California State University, Los Angeles
5151 State University Drive Los Angeles, CA 90032-8160
Tel: (323) 343-4600   Fax: (323) 343-5598
Regularity of Publication: Quarterly
Circulation: 350+ Association Membership   Audited: No
Publisher: Bill Cohen
Editor-in-Chief:James J. Kelly, PhD, MSW, Tel: (323) 343-4600
Advertising Manager: Jackie Blakeslee
Average length of feature: 5-15 pages
How do you prefer your stories to be filed? Send four copies of maunscript to
Dr. Kelly. Prepare copies according to directions in instructions for
authors brochure.

How do you prefer to be contacted? E-mail is best. Phone calls and letters are ok, too.

Special needs of your publication: We are always looking for contributions to our special sections:-book and video reviews-program notes-descriptions or analyses of innovative social service, programs or strategies-news and views-current events and commentary in addition we publish special issues devoted to a single theme. Contact: Dr. Kelly for further information.

What is the best advice for someone contemplating writing for your publication? Consult a recent issue of the journal for instructions to authors.

Journal Of Homosexuality

c/o John P. De Cecco, PhD
Center for Research & Education in Sexuality (CERES),
San Francisco State University Psychology Building, Room 502
San Francisco, CA 94132
Tel: (415) 338-1137   Fax: (415) 824-5380
E-mail: aquinas@sfsu.edu
Regularity of Publication: Quarterly
Circulation: 1400   Audited: No
Publisher: Bill Cohen
Editor: John P. De Cecco, PhD Tel: (415) 338 1137,
E-mail: aquinas@sfsu.edu
Advertising Manager: Jackie Blakeslee
Average length of feature: 5-15 pages
How do you prefer your stories to be filed? By mail
How do you prefer to be contacted? By e-mail
Special needs of your publication: Includes full-length interviews.
What is the best advice for someone contemplating writing for your publication? Read past issues.

JOURNAL OF LESBIAN STUDIES

c/o Esther D. Rothblum, PhD,Professor, Department of Psychology,
John Dewey Hall, University of Vermont,Burlington, VT 05405 0134
Tel: (802) 656 4156   Fax: (802) 656 8783
Regularity of Publication: Quarterly
Circulation: 500   Audited: No
Publisher: Bill Cohen (ext. 329)
Editor: Esther D. Rothblum, PhD

Tel: (802) 656-4156
Assistant Editor: Susan Lillich Tel: (802) 656-4156
Advertising Manager: Jackie Blakeslee (ext. 346)
Average length of feature: 5 - 15 pages
How do you prefer your stories to be filed? By mail
How do you prefer to be contacted? By mail
Special needs of your publication: Empirical and theoretical articles.
What is the best advice for someone contemplating writing for your publication?
Read the instructions for the authors brochure of insert in an issue
of the journal.

Lambda Book Report

PO Box 73910, Washington, DC 20056
Regularity of Publication: Monthly
Phone Number: 202 462 7924   Fax Number: 202 462 5264
E-mail: llf@lambdalit.org
website address: www.lambdalit.org
Publisher and Managing Editor: Jim Marks
Senior Editor: Kanani Kauka
Advertising Director: Robert Costello

The Leather Journal

7985 Santa Monica Boulevard #109-368, West Hollywood CA 90046
Phone 213 656 5073/213 656 3120
E-mail: tljandcuir@aol.com
Publisher and Managing Editor: Dave Rhodes

Lesbian/Gay Law Notes

c/o LeGaL Foundation, 799 Broadway, Suite 340, New York NY 10003
Email: le-gal@interport.net
Regularity of publication: monthly except July
Circulation: approximately 2,000   Audited: No
Phone Number: 212-353-9118   Fax Number: 212-431-1804
(editorial - Art Leonard)
Website Address: www.qrd.org/qrd/www/usa/legal/lgln
Publisher: LeGaL Foundation, Inc., 212-353-9118
Editor: Arthur S. Leonard, 212-431-2156

Circulation: Daniel R. Schaffer, 212-353-9118
Lesbian/Gay Law Notes only publishes writing by its staff members,
and carries no advertising. All writers are volunteers. The editor can
be contacted by email or telephone to discuss editorial content;
inquiries about purchasing back-copies or subscribing should be
directed to the Circulation manager by telephone.

Lesbian Connection

PO Box 811, East Lansing, MI 48826
Regularity of Publication: bimonthly
Circulation: 50,000 Audited: No
Phone Number: 517 371 5257   Fax Number: 517 371 5200
E-mail address: elsiepub@aol.com
Publishers, Editors & Advertising Managers: Ambitious Amazons
How do you prefer your stories to be filed? mail
The writers do not get paid anything. We are a forum of news, &
ideas for, by and about Lesbians. All of our copy is from our readers.
We just put it all together, edit, print and mail it out.

Lesbian News

LN Publishing, P.O. Box 55, Torrance, CA 90507
Regularity of Publication: Monthly
Circulation: 35,0000   Audited: No
Phone Number: 310-7878658 or 562-438-4444
Fax Number: 310-7871965
E-mail address: Theln@earthlink.net
website address: www.LesbianNews.com
Editor in Chief: Claudia Piras--562-438-4444
Average length of feature: 800,1600, or 2500 words
Minimum rate paid per word: (Call editor for current rates)
Minimum rate paid for photos: (Call editor for current rates)
How do you prefer your stories to be filed? Submissions should be sent
by e-mail
How do you prefer to be contacted? We will contact THEM after we receive
submission and if there is interest in the story.
Special needs of your publication: Cartoons, humor, celebrity profiles, cov-

erage of racial minority issues, lesbian views.

What is the best advice for someone contemplating writing for your publication? Pick up one of our magazines, get familiar with it and then submit story ideas you think would be of interest to our readers.

Lesbian Review of Books

PO Box 515, Hilo HI 96721-0515
Regularity of Publication: Quarterly
Circulation: 2500   Audited: No
Phone Number: 808/969-9600   Fax Number: 808/969-7773
E-mail address: loralee@hawaii.edu
Publisher and Editor: Loralee MacPike 808/969-9600
Average length of feature: 2000 words
Minimum rate paid per word: $10 per review
How do you prefer your stories to be filed? We commission most reviews. Inquire if you would like to become a reviewer.
How do you prefer to be contacted? E-mail or regular post.
Special needs of your publication: Would like an ongoing cartoon; would like a lesbian crossword puzzle. Accepts original lesbian poetry.
What is the best advice for someone contemplating writing for your publication? Query us first, telling us what sorts of expertise you have.

Off Our Backs

2337 B 18th Street NW, Washington, DC 20009
Regularity of Publication: Monthly
Circulation: 18-20,000
Phone Number: 202 234 8072   Fax Number: 202 234 8092
E-mail address: offourbacks@compuserve.com
website address: http://www.igc.apc.org/oob/
Average length of feature: Analysis and commentary on current events and trends (local, national, and international) should be about 8 to 10 double-spaced typed pages (about 2000 words). The style should be accessible (please define acronyms, trade terms, etc.).
Minimum rate paid per word: None - Free issues
Minimum rate paid for photos: None - Free Issues
How do you like articles to be submitted? We accept article submission in any format, but much prefer that you send a disk in Word Perfect (any version), Word (any version), or Text/ASCI. The deadline for

54

submissions is the tenth of each month.

How do you prefer to be contacted? Phone or Mail

Special needs of your publication: Off Our Backs accepts a wide variety of materials written from feminist perspectives, including news, analysis, commentary, reviews, and conferences.

What is the best advice for someone contemplating writing for your publication? Reading several issues of the paper is probably the best way to get an idea of the type of material we publish. We are always looking for fresh feminist approaches and viewpoints

ON OUR BACKS

3415 Cesar Chavez Suite 101, San Francisco, CA 94110
Regularity of Publication: Bi-monthly
Circulation: 40,000   Audited: No
Phone Number: 415 648 9464   Fax Number: 415 648 4705
E-mail address: staff@gfriends.com   onourbacks@gfriends.com
website address: www.gfriends.com
Publisher: Erin Findlay
Editor: Athena Douris
Editor in Chief: Heather Findlay
Advertising Manager: Catherine Draper
Average length of feature: 1,000 words
Minimum rate paid per word: varies
Minimum rate paid for photos: $25 and up

How do you prefer your stories to be filed? snail mail

How do you prefer to be contacted? email or snail mail

Special needs of your publication: We're a lesbian sex magazine so we need beautiful, sexy, humorous stories and photos.

What is the best advice for someone contemplating writing for your publication? Read our magazine thoroughly and request a copy of our guidelines before submitting.

Open Hands - Resources for Ministries Affirming the Diversity of Human Sexuality

3801 N. Keeler Ave., Chicago, IL 60641
Regularity of Publication: Quarterly
Circulation: 3000   Audited: No
Phone Number: 773/736-5526   Fax Number: 773/ 736-5475
E-mail address: (Editor's) ChrsGlaser@aol.com

website address: www.rcp.org
Publisher   Mark Bowman 773/736 5526
Editor: Chris Glaser Ph/Fax 404/622-4222 (Atlanta)
Average length of feature: 750-2000 words
Minimum rate paid per word: No payment
Minimum rate paid for photos: None
How do you prefer your stories to be filed? Query first, via e-mail
How do you prefer to be contacted? For subscription, contact publisher in
Chicago; For submissions, e-mail or phone editor in Atlanta
Special needs of your publication: Articles and artwork that fit into thematic
issues related to congregations that welcome l/g/b/t people; check
for themes of upcoming issues
What is the best advice for someone contemplating writing for your publication?
Contact editor and discuss your interest

OUR WORLD MAGAZINE

1104 N. Nova Road #251, Daytona Beach, FL 32117
Regularity of Publication: Monthly
Circulation: 50,000   Audited: No
Phone Number: 904 441 5367   Fax Number: 904 441 5604
E-mail address: info@ourworldmag.com or ourworldmg@aol.com
website address: www.ourworldmag.com
Publisher: Our World Publishing Corp. (ext. 107)
Editor: Wayne Whiston (ext. 101)
editor@ourworldmag.com
Features Editor: (ext. 105)
Arts Editor: (ext. 109)
News Editor: (ext. 210)
Advertising Manager: Jonathan Boardman
904 441 5367 (and main number plus ext. 100) advertising@our-
worldmag.com
Average length of feature: 8,000 words
Minimum rate paid for photos: $200
Special needs of your publication: Travel destinations covering all gay, gay-
friendly hotels, bars restaurants and other practical info.
What is the best advice for someone contemplating writing for your publication? Call
us first

Out & About

350 Seventh Avenue, Ste 1203, New York, NY 10001
or
PO Box 69217, West Hollywood, CA 90069
Regularity of Publication: Monthly with combined issues for
Januray/February and July/August
Circulation: 15,000   Audited: No
Phone Number: 212-645-6922 (pub); 310-859-2774 (editorial)
Fax Number: 212-645-6785
E-mail address: publisher@outandabout; editor@outandabout
website address: www.outandabout.com
Publisher: David Alport
Managing Editor: Billy Kolber-Stuart
Assistant Editor: Ed Salvato
Advertising Manager: Barbara Kolber
Average length of feature: 1500 words
Minimum rate paid per word: $.30
How do you prefer your stories to be filed? electronically
How do you prefer to be contacted? phone or e-mail
Special needs of your publication that freelance writers might be able to fulfill: Call
regarding open assignments
What is the best advice for someone contemplating writing for your publication?
Love to travel. Check out our website and past issues.

Out Magazine

110 Greene Street #600, NY, NY 10012-3838
                              or
Prince Street Station, PO Box 630, New York, NY 10012
e-mail: outmag@aol.com or outpub@aol.com website: www.out.com
Monthly
212 334 9119
Publisher: Louis Fabrizio
Editorial Director: Henry E. Scott
Man Ed   Jolyon Helterman x21
Executive Editor   Tom Beer x16
Dep Ed   Doug Brantley x11
Ed At Large   Lisa Kennedy x19
Advertising Manager   Kurt Demars x33

Contact by mail
Stories of interest to nationwide audience of gay men and lesbians

OUTWord

833 Market St., Suite 511, San Francisco, CA 94103-1824, USA
Regularity of Publication: Quarterly
Circulation: 500   Audited: No
Phone Number: (415) 974-9641   Fax Number: (415) 974-0300
E-mail address: gerardk@asa.asaging.org
Website address: www.asaging.org/lgain.html
Publisher: Lesbian and Gay Aging Issues Network of the American
Society on Aging,   (415) 974-9600
Editor: Gerard Koskovich, (415) 974-9641
Advertising Manager: Nancy Kaplan, Director of Marketing, ASA,
                         (415) 974-9603
Average length of feature: 800 -1,200 words
Minimum rate paid per word: Unpaid
Minimum rate paid for photos: None used
How do you prefer your stories to be filed? Hard copy plus text file.
How do you prefer to be contacted? E-mail.
Special needs of your publication: Exclusive focus on lesbian, gay, bisexual
and transgender aging issues, particularly those of concern to professionals in the field of aging. We run feature stories, first-person
pieces, research summaries, book reviews, resource round-ups, and
event announcements dealing with LGBT aging. Most issues are
organized around a specific theme, such as housing, international
issues, sensitivity training for service providers, etc.
What is the best advice for someone contemplating writing for your publication? Visit
the LGAIN home page at www.asaging.org/lgain.html to review
selected articles from past issues; request author guidelines and
sample issue from editor; query editor about specific needs of the
publication and upcoming issue themes.

PFLAGpole

PFLAG
1101 14th St., NW, Suite 1030 Washington, DC 20005
Regularity of Publication: Quarterly
Circulation: Apx. 80,000 nationwide

Phone Number: 202-638-4200, ext. 212   Fax Number: 202-638-0243
E-mail address: eferrero@pflag.org
website address: www.pflag.org
All inquiries (editorial or advertising) can be directed to: Eric Ferrero
202-638-4200, ext. 212
Average length of feature: 500
How do you prefer your stories to be filed? Generally, we accept submissions
only from PFLAG members or people with specific and relevant
knowledge of PFLAG issues. Submissions should be sent electronically (in the body of an e-mail, not as an attachment) to
eferrero@pflag.org, and mailed to PFLAG at the above address. We
cannot return submissions.
How do you prefer to be contacted? We prefer to be contacted by e-mail or
regular mail.
Special needs of your publication: PFLAGpole's focus is on news
affecting PFLAG chapters, members and supporters, and on family
members and friends of g/l/b/t people in general.
What is the best advice for someone contemplating writing for your publication?
People considering writing for the PFLAGpole should have an in-
depth knowledge of PFLAG's work.

Philogyny:

for women who fuck, suck, stick, lick and love other women

51 Thornton Street, Roxbury, MA 02119
Regularity of Publication: bimonthly
Circulation: 500-1000   Audited:
Phone Number(s): 617-427-2355 or 617-495-6661
E-mail address: philogynyzine@hotmail.com
Publisher: PussyWhipped Publiations: Amie M. Evans 617-427-2355
Editor: Amie M. Evans
Managing Editor: Kristen Porter 617-859-3036 (ext.23)
Advertising Manager: Jean Powers 617-495-6656, 617-523-0194
Average length of feature: 3,000-8,000 words
How do you prefer your stories to be filed? email as part of the body or by mail
How do you prefer to be contacted? email or phone
Special needs of your publication: essays on the social and cultural implica-
tions of lesbians sex, b/f, s/m/d/b, politics of lesbian sex, photos,
erotica, art work, cutting edge work that pushes at the boundaries of
lesbian sexuality
What is the best advice for someone contemplating writing for your publication?

Read lesbian erotica if you intend to write it. Don't be shy in your writing. Show your fantasy. Yes, erotica has a plot. We are willing to work with writers who have good ideas and some talent/skill. Don't send poetry. Consider writing an essay on the politics of lesbian sexuality. Send for guidelines.

Q-Spirit Matters

3739 Balboa Street, Suite 211, San Francisco, CA 94121
Regularity of Publication: Monthly
Circulation: 2500.   Audited: No
Phone Number: 415-281-9377   Fax Number: 415-386-1977
E-mail address: info@qspirit.org
website address: www.qspirit.org
Publisher: Q-Spirit (a nonprofit organization promoting personal growth and spiritual development in the GLBT community)
Editor: Christian de la Huerta 415-386-1145
Average length of feature: 750 words
How do you prefer your stories to be filed? By email, or on PC-formatted disk, in Wordperfect 8.
How do you prefer to be contacted? By email or phone.
Special needs of your publication: We specialize in personal growth and spirituality–very broadly defined, and inclusive of all paths and traditions.
What is the best advice for someone contemplating writing for your publication? Contact editor with story ideas.

qvMagazine

P.O. Box 9700, Long Beach, CA 90810
Regularity of Publication: BiMonthly
Circulation: 15,000   Audited: No
Phone Number: 818.766.0023   Fax Number: 562.696.6595
E-mail address: qvMagazine@aol.com
website address: www.qvMagazine.com
Publisher: Peter Gonzaga
Editor: Demetrio Roldan
Advertising Manager: Peter Gonzaga
Average length of feature: 1000-2000 words
Minimum rate paid per word: Volunteer

Minimum rate paid for photos: Volunteer
How do you prefer your stories to be filed? Sent via e-mail.
How do you prefer to be contacted? Email
Special needs of your publication: Coverage of gay Latino men's issues.
What is the best advice for someone contemplating writing for your publication?
Make sure that submissions are relevant to the gay Latino community. Many submissions to qvMagazine are first-person testimonies.

The SandMUtopian Guardian - A Journal of BDSM Realities

c/o The Utopian Network, POB 1146, NY, NY 10156
Regularity of Publication: Quarterly
Circulation: under 10,000   Audited:No
Phone Number: (516) 842-1711 weekdays 11am-9pm ET
Fax Number: (516) 842-7518
E-mail address: utopian@banet.net
website address: www.aswgt.com
Publishers: Mitch Kessler & Gerrie Blum
Managing Editor: Mitch Kessler
Advertising Manager: Gerrie Blum
Average length of feature: 2000 words
Minimum rate paid per word: $ .03 but prefer to offer per article to avoid "padding."
Minimum rate paid for photos: negotiable when accompanying articles.
How do you prefer your stories to be filed? Hardcopy with accompanying disc in ASCII.
How do you prefer to be contacted? email with phone followup
Special needs of your publication: Book Reviews. National news. News of local groups and organizations. Coverage of racial minority issues. All as related to BDSM.
What is the best advice for someone contemplating writing for your publication?
Think "Popular Mechanix" and "Consumer's Digest." -- Useful, practical factual articles with a BDSM focus. Need not be gender or orientation specific. How to do things, how to make toys and dungeon "funiture," relationships, techniques, how to find partners. A bit of history now and then.

SBC Magazine

A Magazine for Africentric Homosexuals and their Friends

1155 4th Avenue, Los Angeles, CA 90019
Phone 323 733 5661   Fax 323 733 9200
E-mail: sbcmagazine@sprintmail.com
website: www.sbc-online.com
Publisher and Editor in Chief   Stanley Bennett Clay

TOUCHING BODY AND SPIRIT

Box 957, Huntington, NY 11743-1844
Regularity of Publication: Quarterly
Circulation: about 1000,   Audited: No
Phone Number: 1-800-248-3413
E-mail address: sunfire@idt.net
Publisher: Touching Body & Spirit Network
Editor: Sunfire (516) 424-3606
Average length of feature: 2000 words
Minimum rate paid per word: No payment made to contributors
Minimum rate paid for photos: No payment made to contributors
How do you prefer your stories to be filed? E-mail
How do you prefer to be contacted? E-mail, U.S. Postal Service
Special needs of your publication: Our focus is on gay men's spirituality.
We especially welcome articles from workshop leaders and work-
shop participants where the workshop has delt with spirituality for
gay men, and especially erotic spirituality.
What is the best advice for someone contemplating writing for your publication? We
are interested in hearing about your experiences with sacred sex
and your encounters with ultimate reality.

Transformation

Vista Station, P.O. Box 51480, Sparks, NV 89435-1480
Phone: 775 322 5119   Fax: 775 322 6362
Website: www.transformationusa.com
Publisher & Editor: Jeri Lee

Transsexual News Telegraph

41 Sutter Street, #1124, San Francisco, CA 94104-4903
Regularity of Publication: once to twice a year

Circulation: 1,000-5,000   Audited: No
Phone Number: 415.703.7161
Fax Number: 415.775.3848
E-mail address: GailTNT@aol.com
website address: http://members.aol.com/tntwebsite
Publisher/Editor: Gail Sondegaard (415.703.7161)
Assistant Poobah: Katherine Collins
Average length of feature: Varies from 500 to 4,000 words
Minimum rate paid per word: Contributor copies and a gift at
end of year.
Minimum rate paid for photos: Contributor copies and gift at
end of year
How do you prefer your stories to be filed? Via e-mail, but always send a hard
copy. Please be sure your file is in either Word 5.1 or Wordperfect.,
RTF or ASCI format.
How do you prefer to be contacted? Either via e-mail or phone.
Special needs of your publication: Transsexual News Telegraph publishes
specifically for trans.
What is the best advice for someone contemplating writing for your publication?
TNT tries to give its readers analysis and thoughtful feedback on the
reality of living in the world that comes from being trans – that is, living with a very different gender background and reality than most
other people. Significant others, transfans, friends, allies, family
members, are also encouraged to write, as sharing your life with a
transperson is an important part of the trans experience. We are
looking for stories, articles, poems, reviews, and work that is written
from a truthful, personal and honest point of view.

Transgender Community News

c/o Renaissance987 Old Eagle School Road,Suite 719,
Wayne, PA 19087
Regularity of Publication: Monthly
Circulation: 900   Audited: No
Phone Number: 610-975-9119
E-mail address: tcn@ren.org
website address: http://www.ren.org/rnv.html
Publisher: The Renaissance Transgender Association, Inc.
Editor: Angela Gardner editor@ren.orh
Managing Editor: Miranda Wright
Advertising Manager: Gloria Vogel

Average length of feature: 2000 words
Minimum rate paid per word: 1 cent
Minimum rate paid for photos: $25
How do you prefer your stories to be filed? via email in Rich Text Format or mailed on floppy
How do you prefer to be contacted? send query letter via US mail
Special needs of your publication: All of our coverage is related to the transgender community, TS, TV, etc. Stories that have some interest to all members of the TG community are mosty likely to get published. Original cartoons about TG issues are hard to find. We are interested in seeing any that are original art.
What is the best advice for someone contemplating writing for your publication? Understand the TG community or write us a piece on how you view the community.

Trikone

Gay and Lesbian magazine for south-east asians.

P.O. 21354, San Jose CA, 95151, USA
Regularity of Publication: Quarterly
Circulation: 700   Audited No
Phone Number: 415 789 7322   Fax Number: 408 274 2733
E-mail address: publisher@trikone.org
website address: www.trikone.org
Publisher: Khire B V 408 260 8633 publisher@trikone.org
Editor: Sandip Roy 415 285 9182 editor@trikone.org
How do you prefer to be contacted? e-mail

Venus Magazine

P.O.Box 150 Hastings on Hudson, NY 10706
or
(shipping) 785 Warburton AVe. #3 Yonkers, NY 10701
Regularity of Publication: Quarterly
Circulation: 35,000   Audited: Yes-Starting Winter 2000
Phone Number: 914-376-6161   Fax Number: 914-376-1666
E-mail address: editor@venusmagazine.com   venusmag1@aol.com
website address: www.venusmagazine.com
Publisher: Charlene Cothran
Managing Editor: Phil Petrie

64

Features Editor: Phil Petrie
Arts Editor: Kimberly Purnell
Travel Editor: Rosalynd Lloyd
Style Editor: Ernest Montgomery
Health Editor: Steve Wakefield
Advertising Manager: Charlene Cothran
Average length of feature: 1,000 words
Minimum rate paid per word:.20 per word
Minimum rate paid for photos: $20.00 per shot published
How do you prefer your stories to be filed? Text file,or email
How do you prefer to be contacted? email to editor@venusmagazine.com
Special needs of your publication that freelance writers might be able to fulfill:
Lifestyle stories of subjects who happen to be Black gay, lesbian, trans.
What is the best advice for someone contemplating writing for your publication? Get a copy first, look through it then contact us.

WAVES

The Coalition, 800 Village Walk #230 Guilford, CT 06437
Regularity of Publication: quarterly
Circulation: 1,000   Audited: No
Phone Number: 517/855-2277
E-mail address: waves@ecunet.org
website address: http://www.coalition.simplenet.com
Publisher: The United Church of Christ Coalition for Lesbian, Gay, Bisexual and Transgender Concerns   1-800-653-079
Editor: April Allison
Average length of feature: 500-750 words
Minimum rate paid per word: no payment
Minimum rate paid for photos: no payment
How do you prefer your stories to be filed? by e-mail, Word or WordPerfect
How do you prefer to be contacted? by e-mail
Special needs of your publication: Short stories, poems, or news articles are welcome. There should be some connection of the story or the author to the United Church of Christ and to (very broadly defined) lgbt concerns. We are especially interested in the intersections of justice struggles--including antiracism, economic justice, peacemaking, etc.
What is the best advice for someone contemplating writing for your publication? New voices are welcome. Write succinctly and proofread well.

White Crane: A Journal of Gay Men's Spirituality

P O Box 1018, Conifer CO., 80433
Regularity of Publication: Quarterly
Circulation: 400   Audited: No
Phone Number: 303 697 4457
E-mail address: editor@whitecranejournal.com
website address: www.whitecranejournal.com
Publisher/Editor: Toby Johnson
Average length of feature: 2000 words
Minimum rate paid per word: free subscription
Minimum rate paid for photos: no photos
How do you prefer your stories to be filed? pasted into email
How do you prefer to be contacted? email
Special needs of your publication: Thoughtful articles on issues of gay men's spiritual lives. White Crane takes a comparative religions approach (the editor was a student of Joseph Campbell). Book Reviews of relevant material. Travelogues re: pilgrimage spots, holy sites, adventure vacations, etc. No erotica, but we are especially interested in spiritual/psycho-spiritual interpretations of gay sexuality. No news. We do not solicit personal ads from prisoners.
What is the best advice for someone contemplating writing for your publication? Check the website. Subscribe.

Whazzup! Magazine

PO BOX 73648, Washington, DC 20056
Regularity of Publication: Monthly
Circulation: 50,0000   Audited: Yes
Phone Number: 800 962 7024   Fax Number: 718 573 7967
E-mail address: whazzup411@aol.com
website address: Under construction
Editor/Publisher: Stephen Johnson 800 962 7024
Advertising Manager: East 202 483 0472 West 510 836 4759
Rivendell Marketing   (National) 908-232-2021
Average length of feature: 650 words
Minimum rate paid per word: To be negotiated with publisher
Minimum rate paid for photos: To be negotiated with publisher
How do you prefer your stories to be filed? Email submissions
How do you prefer to be contacted? Email

Special needs of your publication: News concerning the African American Gay community.

What is the best advice for someone contemplating writing for your publication?
1. Contact us via email
2. Advise if submission is free or if compensation is requested
3. Follow up on submission
4. Have photos available with story if possible.

XY Magazine

4104 24th St #900, San Francisco, CA 94114-3615
Regularity of Publication: monthly (10x/year, not August/January)
Circulation: 80,000   Audited: Yes
Phone Number: 415 552 6668
Fax Number: 415 552 6664
E-mail address: xymag@aol.com
website address: we have an aol site, keyword XY or
                         www.xymag.com
Publisher: Peter Ian Cummings
Managing Editor: Michael Glatze
News and Features Editor: Benoit Denizet-Lewis
Advertising Manager: advertising hotline 415 552 8666
Average length of feature: all articles are 500-2500 words
Minimum rate paid per word: we pay between $50-$700 per article
Minimum rate paid for photos: $100
How do you prefer your stories to be filed? by email
How do you prefer to be contacted? all queries must be in writing or by email.
XY is the largest national magazine for young gay men.

ALABAMA

R & R Publishing,PO Box 1103, Cullman, AL 35056
Circulation: 1,000 copies (brand new publication)   Audited: No
Phone Number: (256) 775-8488   Fax Number: (256) 775-8498
E-mail address: RnRPublish@aol.com
Publisher: Maranda

ALASKA

P.O. Box 244901, Anchorage, AK 99524
Regularity of Publication: Bi-Monthly
Circulation: 300   Audited or not: NO
Phone Number: 345-3818 (editors)
E-mail address: kk@gci.net klondykeKontact@hotmail.com
Editor: Anne or Barb 345-3818
Advertising Manager: Tami Espy
Average length of feature: 1000 words
Minimum rate paid per word: we do not pay for articles
Minimum rate paid for photos: we do not pay for photos
How do you prefer to be contacted? e-mail
What is the best advice for someone contemplating writing for your publication? Write
something you want to share with Alaskan Women. We publish for
enjoyment. We are Alaska's only Lesbian Newsmagazine. The publi-
cation is sponsored by R.A.W. (Radical Arts for Women), a non-profit

group supporting women in the arts. The Klondyke Kontact is put together by a group of dedicated and amazing volunteers. The Klondyke Kontact is published around the first of the month in February, April, June, August, October, and December. Deadline for submissions is the 15th of the month prior to publication.

Needs: We want news, stories, articles, poetry, art, etc. from Alaska lesbians/bisexuals/feminists. You must give your name, but we can publish your work anonymously if requested.

Length of submissions: For articles, news, and columns, 500 words max. For fiction, features, and/or if we have more space, 1000 words max. Mail your submission to our address or email to kk@gci.net by the 15th of the month deadline date.

Advertising in the Klondyke Kontact

The Klondyke Kontact reaches nearly 500 Alaska lesbian house-holds. We're pretty sure there is no other publication that reaches that many of us and focuses on issues of importance to Alaska lesbians. We'll practically stand on our heads to make you happy advertising in the Klondyke Kontact. Sorry, no free toasters available this month.

NorthView

News and Views for Alaska's Gay and Lesbian Community

P.O. Box 200070, Anchorage, AK 99520-0070
Phone   907 258 4777 888 901 9876
E-mail: identity@alaska.net
website: www.alaska.net/~identity/northview.htm
A publication of Identity, Inc.
Submisions and Deadlines
We welcome articles and letters from community individuals and organizations. Ideal length is 750 words or less. Please submit on 3.5 disk (IBM compatible or MAC HD). All media will be returned. You may also copy your article into the text portion of an e-mail message and send to identity@alaska.net. All contributions must be signed, but upon request names will be withheld or pseudonyms used. NorthView reserves the right to edit as neccessary and to refuse printing of any articles submitted.
All articles must be received by the 5th of the month for inclusion in that month's Northview.
Advertising
Contact NorthView by mail or through the Identity helpline at (907)

258-4777. Advertising may be submitted camera-ready or it can be composed for you in consideration of a negotiated fee. NorthView does not accept Personals, nor does it accept advertising that is sexist, racist, discriminatory or sexually explicit.

THE PERSPECTIVE

SEAGLA
P.O. Box 21542, Juneau, AK 99802
E-mail: seagla@ptialaska.net
Perspective is the monthly newsletter of the Southeast Alaska Gay & Lesbian Alliance. SEAGLA is a nonprofit volunteer organization that provides a support network for lesbian and gay people in Southeast Alaska. SEAGLA aims to foster public acceptance of gay, lesbian, bisexual, and transgendered people as full and equal members of society. Views expressed in Perspective are not necessarily those of SEAGLA or the editorial staff. Articles do not necessarily reflect the sexual orientation of the writer.

SEAGLA makes its mailing list available to other gay/lesbian friendly organizations. Subscribers should contact SEAGLA if they do not wish for their address to be shared with other organizations. Those not wishing to have their information shared will have their identity protected.

Notice to Writers & Graphic Artists:

Perspective welcomes contributions of written and graphic materials for publication. All items must include a name and contact number. Items for publication must be received by the 15th of the month prior to publication. Names can be withheld from publication upon the author's request. The editor reserves the right to modify articles and letters for content, length and clarity.

ARIZONA

Echo Magazine

Ace Publishing Inc., PO Box 16630,Phoenix, AZ 85011-66310
Regularity of Publication: Biweekly
Circulation:18,000   Audited: No

Phone Number: (602) 266-0550 (888) 324 6624
Fax Number: (602) 266-0773
E-mail address: editor@echomag.com
website address: www.echomag.com
Publisher: Bill Orovan
General Manager: Steen Lawson steen@echomag.com
Managing Editor: Bruce Christian
Advertising Manager: Leo Gonzalez
Average length of feature: 1,500 words
Minimum rate paid per word: N/A Paid by story.
Minimum rate paid for photos: $5
How do you prefer your stories to be filed? e-mail
How do you prefer to be contacted? Mail or e-mail
Special needs of your publication that freelance writers might be able to fulfill: We always are looking for hard news stories rather than columns, opinion pieces or entertainment interviews. (It seems everyone wants to write about celebrities, or offer their advice; but no one is covering the news.)
What is the best advice for someone contemplating writing for your publication? Keep it tight. Keep it to the point.

HeatStroke

PO Box 33430,Phoenix, AZ 85067
Regularity of Publication: biweekly (every other thursday)
Circulation: 6-8,000   Audited: No
Phone Number: 602 264 3646 Fax Number: 602 264 3646 (call first)
E-mail address: alkalphx@aol.com or reidhead@idt.net
Publishers: Allen Kalchik & Kelly J. Reidhead
Editor: Allen Kalchik
Managing Editor: Kelly J. Reidhead
Advertising Manager: Kelly and/or Allen
Average length of feature: 1200-1500 words
Minimum rate paid per word: $20-$30 per feature to start
Minimum rate paid for photos: negotiable
How do you prefer your stories to be filed? e-mail or to the P.O. Box
How do you prefer to be contacted? email or mail (Do not fax unsolicited cover letters or samples.)
Special needs of your publication: We're always interested in well-written political essays and in women's issues. Latino/a culture & viewpoints are also of interest. Celebrity profiles must have a gay/lesbian angle

in order to be considered. Regional focus is not a requirement. We don't mind traditionally unpopular political views, provided your point is well made, and we don't shy from controversy.
What is the best advice for someone contemplating writing for your publication?
Know how to write a compelling lead. Know where to put a comma. In short, be able to write. That's about it

Observer

PO Box 50733 Tucson AZ 85703
Phone: 520 622 7176   Fax: 520 792 8382
E-Mail: watcher@azstarnet.com   Editor: Bob Ellis

Rubyfruit Journal

1740 E. Water Street, Tucson, Arizona 85719
Karen Morrison - Editor   akmruby@aol.com
Linda Brawner - Managing Editor   lsdbruby@aol.com
Norma Galindo - Advertising   normag@azstarnet.com
The Journal is always looking for women interested in contributing stories, poems, illustrations, photos, articles, and anything else that might be of interest to the Lesbian community.
Please submit your work using snail mail to:
Rubyfruit Journal - submissions@rubyfruitjournal.com
The Rubyfruit Journal is a Tucson, Arizona based publication dedicated to promoting a sense of community among lesbians whose lives, while quite diverse, are connected by two common threads: the history of oppression and the love of women. Dealing with both issues, the Journal's varied content strives to support and celebrate lesbians, helping to build an even stronger community in which each of our lives will be enriched. If your work is chosen to appear in the Journal you will be emailed a confirmation of inclusion and date of publication as well as a complimentary issue if you are currently not on our mailing list.

CALIFORNIA

Bay Area Reporter

395 Ninth Street; San Francisco, CA 94103-3831
Phone: 415 861 5019   E-Mail: bar@logx.com
http://www.ebar.com
Editor: Cynthia Laird   Asst. Editor: Terry Beswick

The Bottom Line

1243 N. Gene Autry Tr. #121, Palm Springs, CA 92262
Regularity of Publication: biweekly
Circulation: 14,000 per month   Audited: No
Phone Number: 760-323-0552   Fax Number: 760-323-8400
E-mail address: botmline69@aol.com
Publisher: Bill Gordon
Editor in Chief: James Suguitan
Managing Editor: Jim Hooten
Assistant Editor: Jamie O'Neil
Average length of feature: 1000 words
Minimum rate paid per word: negotiable
Minimum rate paid for photos: negotiable
How do you prefer your stories to be filed? email
How do you prefer to be contacted? email
Special needs of your publication: Current events, human interest stories,
national news

creampuff MAGAZINE

199 Duboce Street, San Francisco, CA 94103
Regularity of Publication: Bi-weekly
Circulation: 20,000   Audited: No
Phone Number: 415/554-0565   Fax Number: 415/863-9899
E-mail address: cpmagazine@aol.com
Publisher and Editor: Eric M. Rose
Art Director: Den Legaspi

Calendar Editor: Tom Orr
Office Manager: Joan Jett-Blakk
Advertising Manager: Diana Brown
Average length of feature: 800 words
Minimum rate paid per word: varies
Minimum rate paid for photos: varies
How do you prefer to be contacted? email or mail
Special needs of your publication: interviews, cartoons
What is the best advice for someone contemplating writing for your publication?
We generally seek light-hearted and fun pieces that have somewhat
of an edge or fresh approach to them. We generally publish shorter
pieces, nothing exceeding 1500 words.

fab!

L.A.'s Only Gay and Lesbian Newspaper

6399 Wilshire Blvd., Suite 200, Los Angeles, CA 90048
Regularity of Publication: Biweekly
Circulation: 22,000 Audited: Yes
Phone Number: 323-655-5716   Fax Number: 323-655-1408
E-mail address: fabpub@earthlink.net
Publisher and Editor: Mark Ariel
Managing Editor: Jake Enclan
Features Editor: Yolanda Martinez
Arts Editor: Jake Enclan
News Editor: Yolanda Martinez
Advertising Manager: Mark Ariel
Average length of feature: 500-1500 words
Minimum rate paid per word: $25-$50 per feature
How do you prefer to be contacted? e-mail
Special needs of your publication: Cartoons. Humor. National news. Local
news. Celebrity profiles. Coverage of racial minority issues. Lesbian
news and views.
What is the best advice for someone contemplating writing for your publication? Our
top priority are local items or local features. We are most interested
in investigative reporting on gay issues in Los Angeles. For example:
a recent feature focused on homophobia at a gym in West Hollywood.

4 Front Magazine

7985 Santa Monica Boulevard #69, West Hollywood, CA 90046
Tel: 323 650 7772
e-mail: the4front@aol.com

Frontiers

8380 Santa Monica Blvd.Suite 200, West Hollywood, CA. 90069
Regularity of Publication: Biweekly
Circulation: 76,000   Audited: Yes
Phone Number: 323/848-2222   Fax Number: 323/656-8784
E-mail address: editor@frontiersweb.com or
newseditor@frontiersweb.com or gaynewsla@aol.com
website address: frontiersweb.com
Publisher: Bob Craig(ext. 310)
Editor in Chief: Monica Trasandes (ext.319)
News Editor: Tracy Sypert (ext.330)
Advertising Manager: David Gardner (ext. 321)
Average length of feature: 1,000-1,500 words but are glad to consider longer pieces.
Minimum rate paid per word: Rates vary 5 cents to 10 cents
Minimum rate paid for photos: Rates vary $25-to negotiated on per photo basis
How do you prefer your stories to be filed? Send manuscript via e-mail or regular mail
How do you prefer to be contacted? By mail or e-mail. It can take as long as 4-6 weeks to hear on a story. Please send a SASE if you want your manuscript returned.
Special needs of your publication: Humor is always welcome, would like to run more good, literary fiction (not erotic fiction), always welcome good feature ideas or news features. We're very open to queries and submissions in the following areas: national news, local news, Celebrity profiles, coverage of racial minority issues, Lesbian news and views, although features tend to be more on men's issues since our readership is primarily male.
What is the best advice for someone contemplating writing for your publication?
Make sure you are familiar with what we publish and the style of the writing. Then send writing samples or a story query or the completed story. If you have a story to tell or are a writer who wants a new out-

let for your work, contact us because we are happy to publish sharp, interesting writing.

Gay and Lesbian Times

P.O. Box 34624, San Diego, CA 92163
Regularity of Publication: Weekly
Circulation: 15,000   Audited: NO
Phone Number: (619) 299-6397   Fax Number: (619) 299-3430
E-mail address: gaylt@aol.com
website address: www.gaylesbiantimes.com
Publisher: Michael Portantino
Editor: Bob Findle
Assistant Editor: Janet Saidi
Creative Director: Stephen Vogt
Advertising Manager: Peter Zanni
Average length of feature: words 2,000-2,500
Minimum rate paid per word: varies
Minimum rate paid for photos: varies
How do you prefer your stories to be filed? e-mail
How do you prefer to be contacted? e -mail, no attachments

Holy Titclamps

P.O. Box 590488, San Francisco, CA 94159-0488
e-mail: larrybob@io.com   website: holytitclamps.com

In Magazine

8235 Santa Monica Blvd. #306, West Hollywood, CA 90046-5868
Phone: 323 848 2200   Fax: 323 848 2058
Editor: editor@inlamag.com

The "L" Word

PO Box 272, Bayside, CA 95524
Regularity of Publication: monthly
Circulation: 300   Audited: No
E-mail address: suejh@humbolt1.com

76

Advertising Manager: we're definately not interested in non-local ads
Average length of feature: 300 words
Minimum rate paid per word: (and maximum) $0
Minimum rate paid for photos: same
How do you prefer to be contacted? mail
Special needs of your publication: Mostly local and lesbian, with local and some national lesbian/gay. Local news is mostly events, some book reviews and stories about things that interest us.
What is the best advice for someone contemplating writing for your publication? If you live here and are a lesbian, we'd love to hear from you. If you don't but have something to say to Humboldt county lesbians (and don't expect to get paid for it), we might be interested--write us. We're basically a local paper but we'd like people out there to know we're here in case you're in the neighborhood.

Lavender Godzilla

P.O. Box 421884, San Francisco, CA 94142-1884
Regularity of Publication: Monthly
Circulation: 300   Audited: No
Phone Number: (415)282-4272
E-mail address: gapa@slip.net   website address:slip.net/~gapa
Editor: Dio Gica
Average length of feature: 500 words
How do you prefer to be contacted? e-mail
What is the best advice for someone contemplating writing for your publication? contact us directly by e-mail

The Lavender Reader

P.O. Box 7293, Santa Cruz, CA 95061
Phone: 408 423 8044
Editor: Scottie Brookie (scotty@cruzio.com)
The Lavender Reader is a quarterly magazine for queer folks that some friends and I publish --on paper, not yet online--here in Santa Cruz, California. It's got news and politics and first-person stories and analysis and reviews and fiction (not always all in the same issue) and a sex story (every time). It's 36 pages, usually, on nice paper. We're proud of our cover art, usually created by Bruce Lee.

Manifesto

PO Box 2701, Watsonville, CA 94076-2701
Regularity of Publication: Monthly
Circulation: 3000   Audited: No
Phone Number: 831/761-3176   Fax Number: 831/761-0130
E-mail address: NonHetPapr@aol.com
Publisher and Editor: Mark Krikava, 761-3176
Average length of feature: 500-800 words
Minimum rate paid per word: $0
Minimum rate paid for photos: $0
How do you prefer your stories to be filed? e-mail
How do you prefer to be contacted? e-mail
Special needs of your publication: Local news
What is the best advice for someone contemplating writing for your publication?
small non-profit newspapers rely on volunteers and don't generally
pay for features

MEGA-Scene

611 S. Palm Canyon Dt Suite #7-B, Palm Springs, CA 92264
Phone: 760 327 5178   Fax: 760 323 3646
E-mail: MEGAScene5@aol.com
Publisher & Editor: Bob Hoven

MGW   Mom... Guess What! Newspaper

1725 L Street, Sacramento, CA 95814
Regularity of Publication: Bi-weekly (1st and 15th)
Circulation: 10,000   Audited: No
Phone Number: 916 441 6397   Fax Number: 916 441 6422
E-mail address: info@mgwnews.com
website address: www.mgwnews.com
Publisher & Editor: Linda Birner
Managing Editor: Lee Nichols
Arts Editor: Charles Miller
Advertising Manager: Katherine Davis
Average length of feature: 2,000 words
Minimum rate paid per word: we pay by article

Minimum rate paid for photos: $5
How do you prefer your stories to be filed? e-mail
How do you prefer to be contacted? phone
Special needs of your publication: Cartoons
What is the best advice for someone contemplating writing for your publication? Most of our writers are local.

THE NEXT LA MAGAZINE

7985 Santa Monica Blvd., Suite 207, West Hollywood, CA 90046
Bi-weekly
Circulation: 15,000 per issue   Audited: No
Phone #: 323-656-8118   Fax #:   323-656-6061
E-mail address: Nextla@aol.com
Website address: www.nextla.com
Publisher: Bill Gargani (same number)
Editor: John Price
Advertising Manager: Bobby Kechter
Average length of feature: 1000 to 1500 words
How to be contacted: E-mail or regular mail
Special needs: Celebrity interviews, fictional stories.

Nitelife

1800 N. Hollywood Avenue #604, Hollywood, CA 92028
Regularity of Publication: Biweekly
Circulation: 15,000   Audited: No
Phone Number: 323 462 5400   Fax Number: 323 871 0885
E-mail address: nlmagazine@aol.com or ednitelife@aol.com
Managing Publisher: Michael A Mead 1-888 893 7463
Managing Editor: R. Scott Russell 1-888 893 7463
Entertainment Editor: Dave Depino 323 654 7364
Advertising Manager: K.C. Wilson 323 462 5400
Average length of feature: 500 words
Minimum rate paid per word: 7c
Minimum rate paid for photos: negotiable
How do you prefer your stories to be filed? on disk or e-mail
How do you prefer to be contacted? phone or e-mail
Special needs of your publication: Celebrity profiles
What is the best advice for someone contemplating writing for your publication?

We are a gay entertainment and style magazine. We leave the news and activism to the others.

The Orange County and Long Beach Blade

PO Box 1538, Laguna Beach, CA 92652
Regularity of Publication: Monthly   Audited: No
Phone Number: (949) 494-4898   Fax Number: (949) 494-6945
E-mail address: bladeedtr@aol.com
website address: www.metrog.com (click on Headline News)
Publisher: Bill LaPointe
Editor: Joseph S. Amster
Advertising Manager: Bill LaPointe
Average length of feature: 800-1000 words
Minimum rate paid per word: .05
Minimum rate paid for photos: $15
How do you prefer to be contacted? Phone and email

Out 'N About,

1006 E. Main Street, Suite 100, Ventura, CA 93001
Phone 805-653-1979.
Regularity of Publication: monthly.   Circulation 1000
Average length of features is from 100-200 words.
Stories can be filed by mailing them to the center, either clean copy or diskette (MS Word is the preferred format), or by email to out.n.about@worldnet.att.net.
Special needs: There are no special needs, but local interest articles take precedence. Articles should be submitted before the 10th of the prior month for publication, and we would like to know if the author wishes his/her name to be included (and a phone # to verify).
Editor: Jerry Gray
Advertising Manager: Bobby Nelson

The OuterSider

PO Box 295, Riverside, CA 92502
Regularity of Publication: Monthly
Phone Number: 909-276-1384   Fax Number: 909-276-1384

E-mail address: outersider@hotmail.com
website address: www.outersider.com
Publisher and Editor: John Carlisle 909-276-1384
Average length of feature: 500 words
Minimum rate paid per word: no payment yet
Minimum rate paid for photos: no payment yet
How do you prefer your stories to be filed? electronically (email & attachments)
How do you prefer to be contacted? email first - phone only after email
What is the best advice for someone contemplating writing for your publication? Be familiar with the Inland Empire of Southern California and make it pertinent to the Inland Empire.

OUTNOW Magazine

1020 The Alameda, San Jose, CA 95126
(San Jose and Silicon Valley's Gay and Lesbian Newsmagazine)
Phone: 408 293 1598   Fax: 408 293 1858
Email address: pipervis@ix.netcom.com
Publisher and Editor: Mark Gillard
Managing Editor: Jim Boin
Advertising Manager: Mark Gillard
3/4 page 500 words
Minimum payment per word:10 cents
Minimum payment per phtograph: $25
How do you like to receive contributions: e-mail
How do you like to be contacted: phone or e-mail
Special needs of your publication: local community news, minority news, lesbian news
Out Now encourages individual thought and vision

Outword Newsmagazine

709 28th Street, Sacramento, CA 95816-4116
Regularity of Publication: Biweekly
Circulation: 10,000   Audited: No
Phone Number: 916 329 9280   Fax Number: 916 498 8445
E-mail address: editor@outword.com
website address: www.outword.com or www.outwired.comExecutive
Publisher: Fred Palmer 916 329 9280
                         news@outword.com

Executive Editor: Erich Mathias 916 499 7204
                      editor@outword.com
Arts Editor: Chris Narloch 916 329 9280
                      arts@outword.com
Advertising Sales: Leon Norton 916 499 7204
                      sales@outword.com

Q San Francisco Magazine (QSF)

584 Castro Street, #521, San Francisco, CA 94114
Regularity of Publication: Bi-monthly
Circulation: 49,000+   Audited: NO
Phone Number: 415-764-0324   Fax Number: 415-626-5744
E-mail address: qsf-info@qsanfrancisco.com or qsf1@aol.com
website address: www.qsanfrancisco.com
Publisher: Don Tuthil
Editor-in-Chief: Robert Adams
Features Editor: Steve Cironne
Arts Editor: Stephen Valentino
Advertising Manager: John Maiden
Average length of feature: 3000 words
Minimum rate paid per word: Negotiable
Minimum rate paid for photos: Negotiable
How do you prefer your stories to be filed? electronically
How do you prefer to be contacted? Snail Mail
What is the best advice for someone contemplating writing for your publication?
Send a query letter and at least two writing samples of the kind of
material you wish to submit.

San Francisco Bay Times

3410 19th Street, San Francisco, CA 94110
Regularity of Publication: bi-weekly
Circulation: press run 43,000
Audited: No, but will provide printer's receipts
Phone Number: (415) 626-0260   Fax Number: (415) 626-0987
E-mail address: sfbaytimes@aol.com
Publisher/Editor: Kim Corsaro (ext. 223)
Average length of feature: 1500 words
Minimum rate paid per word: 10 cents

Minimum rate paid for photos: $30
How do you prefer your stories to be filed? via e-mail
How do you prefer to be contacted? phone or e-mail
What is the best advice for someone contemplating writing for your publication? Send in writing samples (preferably published, but not necessary) with a cover letter indicating areas of expertise and writer's special interests. If a writer hasn't been published, write a story on spec in a writing area that interests you (for example, see a movie and review it). We encourage writers' individuality; your writing should reflect your personality to a degree that is appropriate to the material you are writing about. Give time for us to get back to you. Materials won't be returned. A follow-up call after 2-3 weeks is helpful.

San Francisco Frontiers Newsmagazine

2370 Market Street, Second Floor, San Francisco, CA, 94114
Regularity of Publication:Biweekly
Circulation: 30,000   Audited: Yes
Phone Number: 415 487 6000   Fax Number: 415 487 6060
E-mail address: sfnews@frontiersweb.com
                       sfeditor@frontiersweb.com
website address: www.frontiersweb.com
Publisher: Bob Criag
Editors: H. Brock Kolivas, Dino Balzano, Tim Kingston
Managing Editor: H. Brock Kolivas
Features and Arts Editor: Dino Balzano
News Editor: Tim Kingston (ext. 12)
Advertising Manager: H. Brock Kolivas,
Average length of feature: 2,000 words
Minimum rate paid per word: 9 cents
Minimum rate paid for photos: Negotiable
How do you prefer your stories to be filed? on disc or e-mail
Special needs of your publication: We'll take it all.
What is the best advice for someone contemplating writing for your publication?
Know how to write, know how to do a news story, be a competent investigator. Have your own voice. Don't expect us to run a column about your view on the world. We are tired of every queen on the planet thinking they deserve a column.

THE SLANT

PO Box 629, Corte Madera, CA 94925
Published By: THE MARIN STONEWALL ALLIANCE
Managing Editor: Ed Wright
Copy Editor: Carl F. Fye
Production Manager: Mark Nida
Webmaster: Douglas Roper
Regularity of Publication: Monthly
Circulation: 5,500 printed / estimated 12,000 readers
Phone: (415) 924-6635   Fax: (415) 927-3670
Email Address (Printed Edition):   theslant@aol.com
Email Address (For On Line Edition): dbroper@aol.com
Website Address: http://www.theslant.org
How do we prefer stories be filed? By email to "theslant@aol.com" with
attachment in WordPerfect or Microsoft Word;
How do we prefer to be contacted? By phone, by email, by fax
Special needs of your publication: Prefer articles of interest to the GLBT
community of Marin County, California and California in general (our
first priority)--equal weight given to articles of interest to gay men,
lesbians, bisexual/transgender
Best advice for someone contemplating writing to your publication? We are a non-
profit group and the newspaper and website are run entirely by volunteers. At this time, we cannot offer compensation to writers or
contributors. We welcome news, information, articles to those who
are sincere and need a vehicle by which to share their talents.
We are actively seeking advertising for the printed edition as well as
ad banners for the website!

Spectrum

1845 Market Street, San Francisco, CA 94103
Regularity of Publication: Biweekly
Circulation: 20,000   Audited: No
Phone Number: 415-431-1981   Fax Number: 415-252-0724
E-mail address: editor@sfspectrum.org
Website: www.sfspectrum.org
Publisher: David Gin
Editor: Gary Nathan
Features Editor: Sam Rosales

Advertising Manager: Gary Nathan
Average length of feature: 1200 words
How do you prefer your stories to be filed? email
How do you prefer to be contacted? email
Special needs of your publication: Lesbian news and views
What is the best advice for someone contemplating writing for your publication? We
are here for the entire community and want to give a good impres-
sion for us all. We will not take sex ads!

Uncommon Voices (newsletter of BACW)

55 New Montgomery, Ste 321, San Francisco, CA 94105
Regularity of Publication: Bimonthly
Circulation: 1000   Audited: No
Phone Number: 415-495-5393   Fax Number: 415-495-3727
E-mail address: bacw@bacw.org   website address: www.bacw.org
Editor: subject to change (volunteers)
Advertising: contact the main number for info
Average length of feature: 500-750 words
Minimum rate paid per word: we don't pay
Minimum rate paid for photos:we don't pay
How do you prefer your stories to be filed? email attachment-WinWord or text
How do you prefer to be contacted? best to contact the central office for the
current editor.
What is the best advice for someone contemplating writing for your publication? This
is a great place to get some clips if you're just starting out. We are
the newsletter of a non-profit that stresses business and social
events, networking, education and philanthropy, based in the San
Francisco Bay Area. We are always looking for submissions of interest to lesbians: articles, columns, opinion, reviews, art, poetry, fiction.

UPDATE

2801 4th Avenue, San Diego, CA 92103
Regularity of Publication: weekly
Circulation: 15,000 weekly   Audited: No
Phone Number: (619) 299-0500 800 331 1751
Fax Number: (619) 299-6907
E-mail address: Updateed@aol.com

website address: updateonline.com
Publisher: Tom Ellerbrock (Dawn Media)
Editor: Fredric Ball
Managing Editor: Ryan Hurd
Advertising Reps: John Sharkey, Barbara VanDyken
Average length of feature: 1,000 words
Minimum rate paid per word: varies
Minimum rate paid for photos: varies
How do you prefer your stories to be filed? via e-mail
How do you prefer to be contacted? e-mail or phone
Special needs of your publication:
We are a weekly paper serving Southern California
What is the best advice for someone contemplating writing for your publication? We
are the only newspaper format publication in Southern California so
all queries on submissions should be made accordingly.

We the People

P.O. Box 8218, Santa Rosa, CA 95401
Regularity of Publication: Monthly
Circulation: 10,000   Audited: No
Phone Number: 707-573-8896   Fax Number: editorial: 707-569-0972
ads and calendar: 707--527-8384
E-mail address: WTP@aol.com
website address: http://home.pacbell.net/thscribe/wethepeople
Editor: Kory White 707-544-8773,
               thscribe@pacbell.net or vampskater@aol.com
General Manager: 707-527-9753
Average length of feature: 500-750 words
Minimum rate paid per word: $1.75/column inch
Minimum rate paid for photos: $8/photo
How do you prefer your stories to be filed? e-mail
How do you prefer to be contacted? e-mail or phone
Special needs of your publication: features, local and otherwise; local
news, reviews (music, theater, dance, books, art)
What is the best advice for someone contemplating writing for your publication? Just
do it...you have to start somewhere and sometime

COLORADO

H Ink Magazine

1115 Broadway, Suite 105, Denver, CO 80203
Regularity of Publication: Bi-Weekly
Circulation: 8,000   Audited: No
Phone Number: 303-534-4042   Fax Number: 303-534-4407
E-mail address: questh@aol.com
Publisher: Vincent Crowder 303-534-4042
Editor: Alan B. Gentry 303-534-4042 (ext.1)
Advertising Manager: Mark Lundy 303-534-4042 (ext. 2)
Average length of feature: 500-700 words
Minimum rate paid per word: negotiable
Minimum rate paid for photos: negotiable
How do you prefer your stories to be filed? electronic mail
How do you prefer to be contacted? via phone
What is the best advice for someone contemplating writing for your publication?
H Ink Magazine is Denver's party guide for the LGBT Community.
We focus on nightlife, bar scene, gossip, etc. Call our office for more
information.

LesbianPride Newsletter

PO Box 5812, Denver, CO 80217
Regularity of Publication: Monthly
Circulation: varies, less than 1000   Audited: No
Phone Number: 303-286-6533
E-mail address: Morningland@msn.com
Publisher and Editor: Mel White
Editor: Mel White
Average length of feature: 800 words
Minimum rate paid per word: contributor copies
How do you prefer your stories to be filed? typed
How do you prefer to be contacted? mail or e-mail
Special needs of your publication: Short antecdotes, humor, poetry -- all
must be positive, upbeat or inspirational items of general or national
interest; News tidbits, commentary, etc welcome, must be good news

or positive pieces; also publish short pieces about Lesbian businesses and upcoming events.
What is the best advice for someone contemplating writing for your publication? write
for guidelines and a free sample -- I don't print anger or woe-is-me
pieces unless they have a positive twist -- I focus on the positive and
my readers expect to feel good after they read the newsletter about
themselves and each other.

Out Front Colorado

244 Washington St., Denver, CO, 80203
Regularity of Publication: Bi-weekly
Circulation: 40,000   Audited: No
Phone Number: 303.778.7900   Fax Number: 303.778-7978
E-mail address: OutFrontC@aol.com
Publisher and Editor: Greg Montoya
News Editor: John Mandes
Advertising Manager: David Beach
Average length of feature: 500-1,200 words
Minimum rate paid per word: Per story, avg. $35-$100
Minimum rate paid for photos: Included in rate
How do you prefer your stories to be filed? Email w/ backup faxed hardcopy
How do you prefer to be contacted? By telephone
Special needs of your publication: Cartoons, Humor, Book Reviews,
National news, Local news, Celebrity profiles, coverage of racial
minority issues, Lesbian news and views
What is the best advice for someone contemplating writing for your publication?
People's attention span is short. You have to get the reader in, get
them interested, give them the information, and close with them
understanding what the piece was for and about.

Quest Magazine

1115 Broadway, Suite 105, Denver, CO 80203
Regularity of Publication: Monthly
Circulation: 10,000   Audited: No
Phone Number: 303-534-4042   Fax Number: 303-534-4407
E-mail address: Questh@aol.com
Publisher: Vinvent Crowder 303-534-4042
Editor: Alan B. Gentry 303-534-4042 (ext. 1)

Advertising Manager: Mark Lundy 303-534-4042 (ext. 2)
Average length of feature: 70-1500 words
Minimum rate paid per word: negotiable
Minimum rate paid for photos: negotiable
How do you prefer your stories to be filed? e-mail/e-mail attachment
How do you prefer to be contacted? phone
What is the best advice for someone contemplating writing for your publication?
Quest Magazine is Denver's Gay and Lesbian alternative source for news, commmentary, and entertainment information. We do not accept sexually explicit advertising, and our publication works to be all-inclusive.

Connecticut

Metroline

495 Farmington Ave., Hartford CT 06105
Regularity of Publication: Biweekly
Circulation: 16,000   Audited: No
Phone Number(s): 860 233 8334, 888 233 8334
Fax Number: 860 233 8338
E-mail address: info@metroline-online.com   metro493@aol.com
website address: www.metroline-online.com
Publisher: John Crawley   860 231 8845
Editor: James Hall 860 233 8334
Arts Editor: Jamie Houchins 860 233 8336
Advertising Manager: Michael Bogun 860 523 9241
Average length of feature: 700 words
Minimum rate paid per word: negotiable
Minimum rate paid for photos: negotiable
How do you prefer your stories to be filed? email
How do you prefer to be contacted? stories to editor@metronline-online.com
What is the best advice for someone contemplating writing for your publication? We have a low budget.

WAVES

The Coalition,800 Village Walk #230, Guilford, CT 06437
Regularity of Publication: quarterly
Circulation: 1,000   Audited: No
Phone Number: 517/855-2277   E-mail address: waves@ecunet.org
website address: http://www.coalition.simplenet.com
Publisher: The United Church of Christ Coalition for Lesbian, Gay,
Bisexual and Transgender Concerns   1-800-653-079
Editor: April Allison   517/855-2277
Average length of feature: 500-750 words
Minimum rate paid per word: no payment
Minimum rate paid for photos: no payment
How do you prefer your stories to be filed? by e-mail, Word or WordPerfect
How do you prefer to be contacted? by e-mail
Special needs of your publication: Short stories, poems, or news articles
are welcome. There should be some connection of the story or the
author to the United Church of Christ and to (very broadly defined)
lgbt concerns. We are especially interested in the intersections of
justice struggles--including antiracism, economic justice, peacemaking, etc.
What is the best advice for someone contemplating writing for your publication? New
voices are welcome. Write succinctly and proofread well.

DELAWARE

"Letters From CAMP Rehoboth"

39 Baltimore Avenue Rehoboth Beach, DE 19971
Regularity of Publication: Biweekly
Circulation: 7,000   Audited: No
Phone Number: 302-227-5620   Fax Number: 302-227-5604
E-mail address: editor@camprehoboth.com
website address: www.camprehoboth.com
Publisher and Editor: Steve Elkins   302-227-5620
steve@camprehoboth.com
Features Editor: Fay Jacobs   302-227-5620
Arts Editor: Barry Becker   302-227-5620

Advertising Manager: Tricia Massella 302-227-5620
Average length of feature: 1200 words
Minimum rate paid per word: negotiable
Minimum rate paid for photos: negotiable
How do you prefer your stories to be filed? electronically
How do you prefer to be contacted? e-mail
What is the best advice for someone contemplating writing for your publication? We
are a resort area publication and generally prefer features which are
upbeat.

Q Public

Website: www.gaydelaware.com
Circulation: 3,000
Publishers: Gay Delaware
Managing Editor: Denis Crowley   Advertising: Eric Becker

Rehoboth Beach Gayzette

E-mail: rbg@gayrhoboth.com   Website: www.gayrehoboth.com
Published by RBG Publications Inc

DISTRICT OF COLUMBIA

Metro Weekly (MW)

Isosceles Publishing, Inc.
1012 14th Street NW Suite 615, Washington, D.C. 20005
rshulman@metroweekly.net or editor@metroweekly.net
Calendar listings should be directed to calendar@metroweekly.net
Regularity of Publication: Weekly
Circulation: 25,000   Audited: No
Phone Number: 202-638-6830   Fax Number: 202-638-6831
E-mail address: editor@metroweekly.net or mweekly1@aol.com
website address: www.metroweekly.net
Publisher and Editor: Randy Shulman
Assistant Editor: Dan Avery

Advertising Manager: Heather A. Currie
Average length of feature: 2,500 words
Minimum rate paid per word: Do not pay by word.
Minimum rate paid for photos: Negotiable in each situation.
How do you prefer your stories to be filed? Electronically.
How do you prefer to be contacted? Via email.
Special needs of your publication: Book reviews.
What is the best advice for someone contemplating writing for your publication?
Send three samples of your best writing to the editor and follow up in two weeks with a brief phone call. Our feature interviews are typically done in Q&A format.

Off Our Backs

2337B 18th Street NW, Washington, DC 20009
E-Mail: offourbacks@compuserve.com   Website: www.igc.org/oob
Regularity of Publication: 11 times a year
Off our backs is a newsjournal by, for, and about women. It has been published continuously since 1970 -- it is the longest continuously publishing feminist newspaper in the United States. It is run by a collective where all decisions are made by consensus.
The mission of the paper is to provide news and information about women's lives and feminist activism; to educate the public about the status of women around the world; to serve as a forum for feminist ideas and theory; to be an information resource on feminist, women's, and lesbian culture; and to seek social justice and equality for women worldwide.

The Washington Blade

1408 U St., NW Washington, DC 20009-3916
Regularity of Publication: Weekly
Circulation: 46,000   Audited: Yes
Phone Number: 202-797-7000   Fax Number: 202-797-7040
E-mail address: news@washblade.com
website address: http://washblade.com
Publisher: Don Michaels
Editor: Lisa Keen
Managing Editor: Kristina Campbell
Arts Editor: Greg Varner

News Editor: Kristina Campbell
Advertising Manager: Jim Deely
Average length of feature: varies
Minimum rate paid per word: varies
Minimum rate paid for photos: $25
How do you prefer your stories to be filed? e-mail or disk
How do you prefer to be contacted? e-mail or fax
What is the best advice for someone contemplating writing for your publication? Send resume/published samples with query.

Women In The Life

1611 Connecticut Ave NW, Suite B, Washington DC 20009
Monthly
Phone: 202 483 9818   Fax: 202 483 6920
E-mail: witl@usbol.com   Website: womeninthelife.com
Publisher: Sheila A Reid
Editor: Lois Alexander
Advertising Manager: Shakira Washington
Average Length of Feature: 2,000 words
How do you prefer your stories to be filed: e-mail
How do you prefer to be contacted: phone or e-mail
Special needs of your publication: national and local news; lesbian and minority issues
What is the best advice for someone contemplating writing for your publication: Send a sample via e-mail

FLORIDA

Celebrate!

P.O. Box 470, Key West, FL 33041
or   1315 Whitehead, Street Key West, FL 33040
Ciculation: 8,000
Phone: 305 296 1566   Fax:305 296 0458
E-mail: editor@celebrate-kw.com
Publishers: Winston Burrell   publisher@islandnews.com

Community News

PO Box 3725, Tallahassee, FL 32315-3725
Circulation: 15,000   Audited: Yes
Phone Number: 850 425 6397   Fax Number: 850 222 3783
E-mail address: commnews@queerpress.com
Publisher and Editor: Ian Granick

DAVID MAGAZINE

2500 Wilton Drive, Ft Lauderdale, FL 33305
Regularity of Publication: weekly
Circulation: 30,000   Audited: yes
Phone Number: 954- 565-8180   Fax Number: 954-565-8130
E-mail address: aonelitho@aol.com
website address: www.davidmagazine.com
Publisher: Gil Quijas
Editor: Matt Halper
Arts Editor: John Foley
News Editor: Matt Halper
Advertising Manager: David Lee
Average length of feature: 350 words
Minimum rate paid per word: We do not have the need to pay our writers.
Minimum rate paid for photos: depends on the photo for we do most. We have our own photo staff.
How do you prefer your stories to be filed? By content
How do you prefer to be contacted? By phone 954-565-8180
Special needs of your publication: At the current time we are not looking for any new writers.
What is the best advice for someone contemplating writing for your publication?
Contact us directly and submit an article with a background profile.

The Gazette

PO Box 2650, Brandon, FL 33509-2650
Regularity of Publication: Monthly - released the 25th of each month
Circulation: 53,000

Phone Number: 823-689-7566   Fax Number: 813-654-6995
E-mail address: thegazette@aol.com
website address: http://members.aol.com/GazetteOL
Publisher: WORDSplus
Editor: Rand Hall
Advertising Manager: Sue Cummings
Average length of feature: 500-1000 words
Minimum rate paid per word: $10-25 per article
Minimum rate paid for photos: $10
How do you prefer your stories to be filed? Hard copy plus email (included in body of email) or disk (saved as text file only)
How do you prefer to be contacted? email, fax or phone
Special needs of your publication: NEWS and human interest stories only
What is the best advice for someone contemplating writing for your publication? Edit your work for clarity and brevity. Verify and document your facts.

HOTSPOTS!

5100 NE 12th Ave., Fort Lauderdale, FL 33334
Regularity of Publication: Weekly
Circulation:16,000   Audited: No
Phone Number: 954 928 1862   Fax Number: 954 772 0142
E-mail address: hotspots1@aol.com or info@hotspotsmagazine.com
website address: www.hotspotsmagazine.com
Publisher: Jason Bell
Managing Editor: Michael Shelton
Advertising Manager: Kevin LeGrand
How do you prefer your stories to be filed? word "doc" files E-mailed
How do you prefer to be contacted? e-mail
What is the best advice for someone contemplating writing for your publication? submit samples

miamigo Magazine

1234 Washington Avenue, Miami Beach, FL 33139
Regularity of Publication: Monthly
Circulation: 20,000   Audited: No - but it's in the process
Phone Number: 305.532.5051   Fax Number: 305.532.5498
E-mail address: miamigomag@aol   website address: miamigo.com
Publisher: George Mangrum

Managing Editor: Claudia Miller
Advertising Manager: Steve Bodden
Average length of feature: 1,000
How do you prefer your stories to be filed? E-mail
How do you prefer to be contacted? Miamigomag@aol.com
Special needs of your publication that freelance writers might be able to fulfill: We
are in the development and expansion phase. We are in the
process of expanding our distribution to NYC-LA-DC in the next
several months.
What is the best advice for someone contemplating writing for your publication?
Follow deadlines. FYI Miamigo is a full color glossy magazine that
covers Miami but has information on the other major markets in the
US. We average 100 pages and are 81/2 X 11

Ms. DAVID

2500 Wilton Drive, Ft Lauderdale, FL 33305
Regularity of Publication: monthly
Circulation: 14,500   Audited: Yes
Phone Number: 954-565-8180   Fax Number: 954-565-8130
E-mail address: MSDAVID@AOL.com
website address: Currently not up but will be added to the
davidmagazine.com page later this month
Publisher: Gil Quijas
Editor: Joan Nichalson
Managing Editor: David Lee
Arts Editor: Joan Nichalson
Advertising Manager: Ellen Friedman
Average length of feature: 1 1/2 pages words 600
Minimum rate paid per word: we pay by the story
How do you prefer your stories to be filed? by content and thru e mail
How do you prefer to be contacted? phone 954-565-8180
Special needs of your publication: Book Reviews, National news, Celebrity
profiles, Lesbian news and views,
What is the best advice for someone contemplating writing for your publication?
Contact us directly.

SCOOP

2205 Wilton, Drive Wilton Manors, FL 33305

Phone 954 561 9707   Fax: 954 561 5970
E-mail: scoop@scoopmag.com   Website: www.scoopmag.com
Publisher & Editor: Brad Casey

She Magazine-The Source For Women

2205 Wilton Drive, Ft. Lauderdale, FL 33305
Regularity of Publication: Monthly
Circulation:10,000   Audited: No
Phone Number:954-561-9707   Fax Number: 954-561-5970
E-mail address: shemag@mindspring.com
website address: http://www.shemag.com
Publisher: Brad Casey, Scoop Publishing
Editor: Karen Campbell - 954-954-8418
Production Manager: Tina Sordellini
News Editor: Tony Ramos
Advertising: Tina Sordellini 954-478-2196 or Natalie Lantz
Average length of feature: 900-1000 words
How do you prefer your stories to be filed? e-mail
How do you prefer to be contacted? e-mail

Southern Exposure Guide

819 Peacock Plaza #575 Key West FL 33041
Phone: 305 294 6303 E-mail:feedback@kwest.com
www.kwest.com
monthly
Editor: Jon McConnell

TLW Magazine (The Last Word)

PO Box 60582, Jacksonville, FL 32236
Published twice monthly on the 7th and the 21st
5,000 copies printed at each press run (not audited) TLW is distributed from Atlanta to Key West to New Orleans...with our heaviest circulation in south GA and North and Central Florida including
Jacksonville, Tampa, Orlando, and Daytona Beach
Phone: 904-384-6514   Fax: 904-378-9856

Email: Tlastword@aol.com
Web: www.tlwmen.com (currently under construdtion)
Publisher: Ron Fields pager: 888-705-0623 or
office phone above
Ron Fields should be contacted for any information including adver-
tising, articles, etc.
TLW is in it's 6th year of publication and is an entertainment maga-
zine/bar guide catering to the gay male.
Based in Jacksonville, Florida 5 years old For Men By Men With
Men In Mind We're a men's entertainment magazine, check us out
Check out our Website! www.TLWMEN.com
Publishers Ron Fields & Art B. Taboada

TWN: South Florida's Gay Community Newspaper

901 NE 79th St, Miami, FL 33138
Phone 305.757.6333   Fax 305.756.6488
Email   bwatson@theweeklynews.org
website: www.theweeklynews.org
Weekly
Publisher: Bill Watson

Watermark

414 N. Ferncreek Ave., Orlando, FL 32803
Regularity of Publication: weekly
Circulation: 20,000   Audited: No
Phone Number: (407) 481-2243   Fax Number: (407) 481-2246
E-mail address: editor@watermarkonline.com
website address: watermarkonline.com
Publisher& Editor: Tom Dyer (407) 648-1153
Tom@watermarkonline.com
Managing Editor: (407) 481-2243 x.11
Features Editor: (407) 481-2243 x.12
Arts Editor: (407) 481-2243 x.19
News Editor: (407) 481-2243 x.19
Advertising Manager: Ken Worth (407) 481-2243 x.14
Average length of feature: 1250 words
Minimum rate paid per word: 5 cents/word
Minimum rate paid for photos: $20/photo
How do you prefer your stories to be filed? e-mail, in MSDos Text

How do you prefer to be contacted? e-mail
Special needs of your publication: Cartoons, Humor, Book Reviews, National news, only local news, Celebrity profiles, coverage of racial minority issues, Lesbian news and views, investigative pieces, think pieces.
What is the best advice for someone contemplating writing for your publication? Contact via e-mail with sample.

GEORGIA

Etcetera magazine

151 Renaissance Pkwy., Atlanta, GA 30308
or P.O. Box 8916 Atlanta GA 30306
Regularity of Publication: Weekly
Circulation: 23,000 Yes - ABC
Phone Number: 404-888-0063   Fax Number: 404-888-0910
E-mail address: Etc@mindspring.com
website address: www.etcmag.com
Publisher: James Heverly
Editor: Jack Pelham
Features Editor: Jack Pelham
Arts Editor: Jack Pelham
News Editor: Rob Nixon
Advertising Manager: Ron Whalen
Average length of feature: 1,200 words
Minimum rate paid per word: .06 cents
Minimum rate paid for photos: $25
How do you prefer your stories to be filed?   e-mail
How do you prefer to be contacted?   e-mail or phone
Special needs of your publication: 99.9% queer content
What is the best advice for someone contemplating writing for your publication? E-mail or fax story.

Southern Voice

1095 Zonolite Road, Suite 100, Atlanta, GA 30306
Regularity of Publication: weekly

Circulation: 30,000   Audited: No
Phone Number: 404-876-1819   Fax Number: 404-876-2709
E-mail address: southvoice@aol.com;
website address: www.southernvoice.com; www.sovo.com
Publishers: Chris Crain (ext. 22)
                 Rick Ellsasser (ext. 23)
Editor: Chris Crain (ext. 22)
Managing Editor: Matt Hennie (ext. 18)
Advertising Manager: Bob Mathis (ext. 15)
Average length of feature: 1200 words
Minimum rate paid per word: .07
Minimum rate paid for photos: $15
How do you prefer your stories to be filed? hard copy, plus electronic
How do you prefer to be contacted? letter
What is the best advice for someone contemplating writing for your publication? Send writing samples with queries. If you want anything returned, send SASE. Do not expect immediate response.

TIMELESS VOICES

P.O. Box 23697, Macon, GA 31212-3697
Regularity of Publication: Quarterly
Circulation: 2,000   Audited: No
Phone Number: 912-744-9681   Fax Number: 912-744-6364
E-mail address: timelessvoices@onmacon.com
website address: http://onmacon.com/pride
Publisher: Timeless Voices 912-744-9681
Editor: Elle Hills 912-744-9681
                 wildvirgogirl@onmacon.com
News Editor: Chris Coggins 912-744-9681
Advertising Manager: Chris Coggins 912-744-9681
Average length of feature: 250 words
Minimum rate paid per word: 0
Minimum rate paid for photos: 0
How do you prefer your stories to be filed? Via e-mail/text attatchment
How do you prefer to be contacted? Via e-mail
Special needs of your publication: Primarily we focus on LGBTF living in middle/south Georgia.
What is the best advice for someone contemplating writing for your publication? Contact us first for space availability.

100

HAWAII

OG Magazine

OG Magazine (USA) 1164 Bishop St. #124-293, Honolulu, HI 96813
Regularity of Publication: quarterly
Circulation: 10,000   Audited: No
Phone Number: 808-526-3742   Fax Number: 808-526-3742
E-mail address: ogusa@lava.net
website address: www.ogusa.com
Publisher and Editor: Edward Chew
Advertising Manager: Peter Sturges
Average length of feature: 500 words
How do you prefer to be contacted? email
What is the best advice for someone contemplating writing for your publication? gay
asian erotica.

OUT IN MAUI

PO Box 5042, Kahului, HI 96733-5042
Regularity of Publication: Monthly
Circulation: 2000   Audited: No
Phone Number:808 244 4566   Fax Number: 808 248 7501
E-mail address: gaymaui@maui.net
Publisher: Both Sides Now Inc
Editor: Richard F. Wahl
Advertising Manager: Bob Kerr 244 4566
Average length of feature: 500 words
Minimum rate paid per word: 0
Minimum rate paid for photos: 0
How do you prefer to be contacted? Phone

OUTSPOKEN

PO Box 1746, Pahoa, HI 96778
Regularity of Publication: Quarterly
Circulation: 700   Audited: No

Phone Number: 808/965-4004
E-mail address: buck@bigisland.com
website address: www. aesweb.com/out
                     (soon to be...outinhawaii.com)
Publisher and Editor: P.F. Buck   808/965-4004
How do you prefer to be contacted? email
What is the best advice for someone contemplating writing for your publication?
don't bother unless you have first hand Hawaii experience to share. I
just can not stress enough that we are focused on the local queer
community on the big island.

IDAHO

Diversity News

919 27th, Boise, ID 83702
or
P.O. Box 323, Boise, ID 83701-0323
Regularity of Publication: Monthly (Except January)
Circulation: 2,000 Audited: No
Phone Number: Message 208-336-3870 Mailbox 2
Fax: (208) 323-0805
E-mail: DiversityN@aol.com (not for correspondence)
E-mail address: thepaper@micron.net
website: www.geocities.com/WestHollywood/Village/2428
Publisher: The Gay & Lesbian Community Center
Editor: Michael Healy
Advertising: Wil Dyal
News Editor: Rich Keefe
Calendar Editor: Teresa Wood
Minimum rate paid per word: Non-profit organization -- does not pay
for submissions
Minimum rate paid for photos: Non-profit organization -- does not
pay for submissions
How do you prefer your stories to be filed? e-mail
How do you prefer to be contacted? e-mail
Special needs of your publication: paper is done entirely by volunteers.
Submissions must be received by the 15th of the month preceeding
publication.

ILLINOIS

BUTI VOXX Magazine

5120 So. Harper Ave., Flat A-7, Chicago, Illinois 60615
Regularity of Publication: During Black Lesbian & Gay Conferences/
Pride Celebrations
Circulation: 500 - 750 per issue   Audited: No
Phone Number: 773.752.5348
E-mail address: Butivoxx59@aol.com
Publisher: Gregory D. Victorianne 778.752.5348
Average length of feature: 750 words
Minimum rate paid per word: zero
Minimum rate paid for photos: zero
How do you prefer to be contacted? E-mail
Special needs of your publication: Cartoons, Humor, Book Reviews,
National news, local news, Celebrity profiles, coverage of racial
minority issues, lesbian news and views. Allow yourself to be one of
the person's who have allowed our voices to be heard / recorded
and remembered.

Chicago Free Press

3714 N. Broadway, Chicago, IL 60613
Regularity of Publication: Weekly
Circulation: 26,000   Audited: Yes
Phone Number: (773) 325-0005   Fax Number: (773) 325-0006
E-mail address: news@chicagofreepress.com
website address: www.chicagofreepress.com
Publisher: Novus Publishing Group
Editor-in Chief: Louis Weisberg
Managing Editor: Lisa Neff
Features Editor: Lisa Neff
Arts Editor: Jen Earls
News Editor: Lisa Neff
Advertising Manager: Mark Olley
Average length of feature: 1,200 words
How do you prefer your stories to be filed? electronically

How do you prefer to be contacted? email

Special needs of your publication: Chicago Free Press has a staff of three editors/writers and several regular columnists/reviewers. So what we look for are off-beat, extraordinary enterprise stories—news features, profiles, travel journals, entertainment interviews.

What is the best advice for someone contemplating writing for your publication? Pitch the unusual and write stories that pop. Also, we're a newspaper, so we don't publish "I" pieces—essays, short stories and poems.

GAB Magazine

3227 N. Sheffield, 4th Floor rear, Chicago, IL 60657
Phone 773 248 4542 (main)   773 477 6179 (music department)
e-mail: gabmag@earthlink.net
Circulation: 18,000   Audited: No
Publisher   Propago Publishing Malone Sizelove
Editor   Jim Pickett
Music editor   Freddie Bain
Arts editor   Lee Gerstein
Advertising Manager   Jim Pickett
Length of feature: 750 words
negotiated
Stories files via fax or e-mail
Prefer to be contacted phone/snail mail
Advice to future Gab contributoes - have an idea and send us a sample

Gay Chicago Magazine

3121 N. Broadway, Chicago IL 60613
Regularity of Publication: weekly
Circulation: 20,000   Audited: No
Phone Number: 773 327 7271   Fax Number: 773 327 0112
E-mail address: gaychimag@aol.com
website address: www.gaychicago.com
Publisher: Ralph   Paul Gernhardt gaychirpg@ao.com
Features Editor: Jeff Rosen
News Editor: Jerry Williams jfwiliams@aol.com
Advertising Manager: Mark Nagek
Minimum rate paid for photos: done by staff
How do you prefer your stories to be filed? e-mail

How do you prefer to be contacted? e-mail
Special needs of your publication: Cartoons, Humor, Book Reviews,
National news, local news, Celebrity profiles, coverage of racial
minority issues, Lesbian news and views.
What is the best advice for someone contemplating writing for your publication?
Send it in.

Outlines (weekly)

1115 West Belmont, Suite 2-D, Chicago, IL 60657
Nightlines (weekly)   BLACKlines (monthly)
En La Vida (monthly)   Clout! Business Report (quarterly)
OUT! Resource Guide (twice per year)
Taste (dining guide, quarterly)
Circulation:
Outlines (20,000 weekly)   Nightlines (12,000 weekly)
BLACKlines (10,000 monthly)   En La Vida (6,000 monthly)
Clout! Business Report (5,000 quarterly)
OUT! Resource Guide (25,000 twice per year)
Taste (15,000 dining guide, quarterly)
Audited: NO
Phone Number: 773-871-7610   Fax Number: 773-871-7609
E-mail address: outlines@suba.com
website address: www.outlineschicago.com
Publisher & Managing Editor: Tracy Baim (ext.17)
Average length of feature: 600-1500 words
Minimum rate paid per word: pay per article $20-$50
Minimum rate paid for photos: $5-$20
How do you prefer your stories to be filed? e-mail, into the message itself,
not attached
How do you prefer to be contacted? e-mail
Special needs of your publication: Cartoons, national and local news,
celebrity, leader profiles, leader interviews
What is the best advice for someone contemplating writing for your publication? send
into e-mail message 3-4 samples of writing, or send via snail mail.
Then contact via e-mail with specific story ideas.

Prairie Flame

P. O. Box 2483, Springfield, IL 62705-2483 (118B E. Laurel)

Regularity of Publication: Monthly
Circulation: Print run normally 5,500   Audited: No
Phone Number: 217/753-2887   Fax Number: 217/753-4209
E-mail address: pflame@eosinc.com
Publisher and Editor: Buff Carmichael
Advertising Manager: Buff Carmichael
Average length of feature: 500 words
Minimum rate paid per word: have not yet purchased any feature
Minimum rate paid for photos: have not yet purchased any photos
except local
How do you prefer your stories to be filed? e-mail
How do you prefer to be contacted? e-mail
Special needs of your publication: Horoscope column, cartoons
What is the best advice for someone contemplating writing for your publication?
When your priority is to make others aware, we are interested in
helping. When your priority is to receive a check and/or sell a prod-
uct, we are entirely too small and too new to have the resources to
comply. We do appreciate receiving submissions, but have not yet
begun purchasing any of them.

WINDY CITY TIMES

325 W. Huron, Suite 510, Chicago, Illinois 60610
Editorial (312) 397-0025   Advertising (312) 397-0020
Fax (312) 397-0021
Publisher and Editor: Jeffrey McCourt editorial@wctimes.com

INDIANA

The Bloomington Beacon

P.O. Box 3307, Bloomington, Indiana 47402
Regularity of Publication: Monthly
Circulation: 7,000+   Audited: No
Phone Number: (812) 336-2533   Fax Number: (812) 335-1473
E-mail address: Newbeacon@aol.com
Publisher: Bloomington Beacon, Inc. (a 501c3 non-profit corporation)
Editor: John W. Clower (812) 336-2533

Features Editor: Fran Record
Arts Editor: Steve Yandell
News Editor: R. O. Lake
Advertising Manager: Daniel Soto
Average length of feature: 600 words
Minimum rate paid per word: All copy is volunteer written
Minimum rate paid for photos: All photos are contributed
How do you prefer your stories to be filed? electronically
How do you prefer to be contacted? by phone or e-mail
What is the best advice for someone contemplating writing for your publication? The Beacon is an all-volunteer run, not-for-profit publication serving the GLBT communities of south-central Indiana, western Ohio, and northern Kentucky. We are always interested in stories and features that touch the lives of queerfolk living in this geographical area. The paper was founded to provide a better source of news and information to the queer community than was being offered by the local area "bar rag." We welcome well-written, contributed articles and publishable photos, but current budgetary constraints make it impossible for us to pay for such materials.

IXE Newsletter

IXE, PO Box 20710, Indianapolis, IN 46220
Regularity of Publication: monthly
Circulation: ~100   Audited: No
Phone Number(s): 317-971-6976   E-mail address: ixe@aol.com

website addresses:
http://www.geocities.com/WestHollywood/Stonewall/5745   or
http://www.gayindy,org/ixe or http://members.aol.com/ixe/fish/
Publisher: IXE   Non-profit gender support group newsletter
Minimum rate paid per word: we do not pay for articles
Minimum rate paid for photos: we do not pay for photos
How do you prefer your stories to be filed? e-mail
How do you prefer to be contacted? via e-mail
Special needs of your publication: We are a newsletter for a gender support group

OUTlines, The Indiana Gay & Lesbian Newsmagazine

133 W. Market Street, Suite 105, Indianapolis, IN 46204-2801
Regularity of Publication: Monthly
Circulation: 20,000 per month (2,000 by mail)   Audited: No
Phone Number: 317 923 8550   Fax Number: 317 923 8505
E-mail address: editor@indygaynews.com
website address: www.indygaynews.com
Publisher and Editor   Bruce Seybert 317 923 8550
Average length of feature: 500-700 words
Minimum rate paid per word: inquire
Minimum rate paid for photos: inquire
How do you prefer your stories to be filed? sent by e-mail
How do you prefer to be contacted? by phone
Special needs of your publication: news, features, articles pertaining to inside Indiana or that have an Indiana connection or angle.

The Rainbow Reader

Up The Stairs Community Center;
3426 Broadway; Fort Wayne, IN 46807
Regularity of Publication: Monthly
Circulation: 1500   Audited: No
Phone Number: (219) 744-1199 (evenings only)
E-mail address: rainbow@fwi.com
website address: http://www2.fwi.com/~rainbow
Staff is all-volunteer - no paid staff.
Average length of feature: 1200   words
Minimum rate paid per word: do not pay
Minimum rate paid for photos: do not pay
How do you prefer your stories to be filed? Word
How do you prefer to be contacted? email
Special needs of your publication: We do a pretty decent job on everything considering our volunteer nature. We have always wanted to add some humor, but since we're not able to pay for submissions we haven't done anything.
What is the best advice for someone contemplating writing for your publication?
We are a 'break-even' operation. The more advertisers we have, the more paper we have. Unsolicited articles are included as space is available (which IS somewhat common). The editorial staff are

sticklers on proper spelling, grammar and punctuation.

The Word

(editions for Indiana, Ohio & Kentucky)
501 Madison Ave., Suite 307, Indianapolis, IN 46225-1109.
Regularity of Publication: monthly
Circulation: 14,000+
Audited: No, but notarised printer letter is available upon request.
Phone Number: 317 725.8840   Fax Number: 317 687.8840
E-mail address: indword@iquest.net
website address: http://www.indword.com AND
                         http://www.ohioword.com
Publisher: Ted Fleischaker, who will handle ALL calls on
all topics and transfer caller as needed. Direct line is listed above.
Minimum rate paid per word: Pay as agreed by the feature/story.
How do you prefer to be contacted? We dont....we have all the copy and info
we need from our network of local writers & longtime established DC
and other people. Nothing more is needed.
What is the best advice for someone contemplating writing for your publication? Dont
bother at this time...we are being solicited like crazy and do not
need or buy anything...please save the time & postage and dont
write or ask! We trash all queries as we have a LOCAL and
REGIONAL interest which is why we are wildly successful. We do
not purchase anything outside except longtime, established writers
who we already have.

IOWA

ACCESSline

317 Hartman Avenue, Waterloo, Iowa 50701-2332
Regularity of Publication: bimonthly
Circulation: 3000 across Iowa, expecially in eastern section.
(400 subscriptions)
Phone Number: 319-232-6805   E-mail address: access@forbin.com
Publisher: Les Davis, President ACCESS in NE Iowa.
                   (319)232-6805
Editor: John T. Wilson   (319) 232-6905

Arts Editor: Ron Evans   (319)232-6805
Advertising Manager: Paul Danielsen (319) 232-6805
Average length of feature: 600-1800 words
Minimum rate paid per word: seldom buy articles; all volunteer staff;
up to $20
Minimum rate paid for photos: $5 and up
How do you prefer your stories to be filed?
email marked ARTICLE SUBMISSION
How do you prefer to be contacted? email
Special needs of your publication: Prefer local Iowa writers, but like solid,
creative work treating a variety of subjects. Essays and editorials
welcome. Human interest pieces(i.e. personal stories) also ok.
Reviews also considered.
What is the best advice for someone contemplating writing for your publication?
Send sample work for consideration: prefer included in email, with
publication information. Attached file should be in common format
(rich text format, word perfect, microsoft word).

Iowa's Pride

The University of Iowa
SAC / Iowa Memorial Union Iowa City, IA 52242-1317
Regularity of Publication: Monthly (9 issues/academic year)
Circulation: 2,000   Audited: No
Phone Number: 319-335-3251   Fax Number: 319-335-3407
E-mail address: iowa-pride@uiowa.edu
Website address: http://www.uiowa.edu/~iapride
Editor: Cat Berry, 319-335-3251
Managing Editor: Dan Sydnes, 319-335-3251
Advertising Manager: Charles Dufano, 319-335-3251
Average length of feature: 750-1250 words
How do you prefer your stories to be filed? Mail or E-mail Attachment
How do you prefer to be contacted? Phone or E-mail
Special needs of your publication: Cartoons, humor, opinion, mostly
local/state news, some national news, book/music/video reviews,
photography
What is the best advice for someone contemplating writing for your publication? Hard
copy submissions (photography, art, printed matter) can be mailed to
the address above. All other submissions may be sent as e-mail
attachments. Works from University of Iowa students, staff, and fac-
ulty receive priority consideration. Submission deadline is the 15th

110

of every month.

OUTword

414 E. 5th St., Des Moines, IA 50309-7008
E-Mail outword414@aol.com   website: www.serve.com/glrc
OUTword is a bi-monthly newspaper published by the GLRC. It
informs the community of news, features, events, and contains
advertisements by gay-owned and supportive businesses throughout
central Iowa. OUTword is mailed free to all GLRC members, and is
available for free at several nightclubs, coffeehouses, bookstores,
and other establishments around Des Moines.

KANSAS

The Liberty Press

PO Box 16315, Wichita, KS 67216-0315
Regularity of Publication: Monthly
Circulation: 6,000   Audited: No
Phone Number: (316) 652-7737; In Topeka: (785) 267-2991;
In Lawrence: (785) 842-7714
Fax Number: (316) 685-1999
E-mail address: editor@libertypress.net; In Topeka or Lawrence:
laweditor@libertypress.net   website address: www.libertypress.net
Publisher: The Liberty Press, Inc.
Editor: Kristi Parker
Managing Editor: Sharon Faith Levin
Advertising Manager: Vinnie Levin in Topeka
or in Lawrence: Kristen Wiebe
Average length of feature: 1000-1200 words
Minimum rate paid per word: none
Minimum rate paid for photos: none
How do you prefer to be contacted? by mail
Special needs of your publication: only local news - based in Kansas
What is the best advice for someone contemplating writing for your publication? All of
our writers are volunteer! We carry very few syndicates.

The Triangle

P.O. Box 11347 Wichita, KS 67202
Phone 316 267 1991   e-mail: editor@trianglemag.com
website: www.trianglemag.com
monthly
General Manager: Chuck W. Breckenridge

The Vanguard

423 Kansas Union,University of Kansas Lawrence, KS 66044
Regularity of Publication: Monthly
Circulation:local (Lawrence, KS/ University of Kansas)   Audited: No
Phone Number: 864-3091
E-mail address: qanda@raven.cc.ukans.edu
Editor: Matthew Skinta
Average length of feature: 10 pages words/page: 1600
Minimum rate paid per word: none
Minimum rate paid for photos: none
How do you prefer your stories to be filed? hardcopy or e-mail is fine
How do you prefer to be contacted? e-mail to: quiddity@eagle.cc.ukans.edu
Special needs of your publication: All types of submissions are welcome.
Though general themes are chosen for each issue and the submissions chosen in accordance, all topics of concern to the queer community, local or national, are welcome.
What is the best advice for someone contemplating writing for your publication? Be concise, clear, and try to keep your stories on a very personal level. Being only a locally circulated work, printed by the University, I try as editor to make it as accessible as possible to whomever might pick it up.

KENTUCKY

The Letter

PO Box 3882, Louisville, KY 40201
Regularity of Publication: Monthly

Circulation: 17,000 readership
Phone Number: 502/636-0935 (news & administration)
                                 502/772-7570 (advertising)
                                 502/895-7711 (web page/web advertising)
Fax Number: 502/635-6469
E-mail address: WillNich@aol.com
website address: www.iglou.com/theletter (this will change in '99)
Publisher: Phoenix Hill Enterprises, Inc., 502/636-0935
Editor: David Williams, 502/636-0935
Arts Editor: David DewBerry, 812/284-3448
Advertising Manager: Jeff, 502/772-7570
Average length of feature: 1,000 words
Minimum rate paid per word: $15 for all
Minimum rate paid for photos: $5
How do you prefer your stories to be filed? **Email**
How do you prefer to be contacted? **Email**
Special needs of your publication: **General**
What is the best advice for someone contemplating writing for your publication?
Feature writers should find a different or unusual angle and should write with pizazz.

LOUISIANA

Ambush Mag

828-A Bourbon St., New Orleans, LA 70116-3137
Regularity of Publication: Biweekly
Circulation: 10,000   Audited: No
Phone Number: 504.522.8049   Fax Number: 504.522.0907
E-mail address: webmaster@ambushmag.com
website address: www.ambushmag.com
Publisher: Rip Naquin-Delain
Editor: Rip Naquin-Delain
Managing Editor: Sonny Cleveland
Arts Editor: George Patterson
News Editor: George Patterson
Advertising Manager: Sonny Cleveland
Average length of feature: 700 words
Minimum rate paid per word: $25 per column

Minimum rate paid for photos: $10 per photo
How do you prefer your stories to be filed? via email
How do you prefer to be contacted? via email
Special needs of your publication: interested in news, especially lesbian news and views, plus coverage of racial minorities.

Impact News

2118 Burgundy St., New Orleans, La. 70116
Regularity of Publication: biweekly, going weekly this year
Circulation: 21,000 per issue
Phone Number: 504.944.6722   Fax Number: 504.944.6794
E-mail address: gaymail@impactnews.com
website address: www.impactnews.com
Publisher: Rick Ellsasser 404.876.1819 [Atlanta, Ga. office] (ext. 23)
Editor: Melinda Shelton   504.944.6722
          editor@impactnews.com
Arts Editor: Lucas Mire 504.944.6722
Advertising Manager: Mike Theis 504.944.672
Average length of feature: 800 words
Minimum rate paid per word: paid per article
Minimum rate paid for photos: no set rate, depends on topics
How do you prefer your stories to be filed? email and disk
How do you prefer to be contacted? telephone, fax
Special needs of your publication: Stories, cartoons, humor items, features of interest to our Gulf Coast readers
What is the best advice for someone contemplating writing for your publication?
Contact the editor by telephone and be prepared to submit samples via email, fax, or mail. It is very helpful to have art with the story.

MARYLAND

The Baltimore Alternative

P.O. Box 2351, Baltimore, MD 21203
UPS Address: 36 W. 25th Street, Baltimore, MD 21218
Regularity of Publication: Biweekly
Circulation: 40,000 readers   Audited: No

Phone Number: 410-235-3401   Fax Number: 410-889-5665
E-mail address: baltalt@aol.com   website address: baltalt.com
Publisher: Charles Mueller (ext. 10)
Editor: Paula Langguth Ryan (ext. 11)
Arts Editor: D.C. Culbertson (ext. 17)
News Editor: David Baker (ext. 15)
Advertising Manager: Don Peacock (ext. 12)
Average length of feature: 1200-3400 words
Minimum rate paid per word: $10-$50 total depending on article
Minimum rate paid for photos: $20/photo
How do you prefer your stories to be filed? electronically as RTF attachment.
How do you prefer to be contacted? via email or snail mail
Special needs of your publication: Book Reviews, Local news, Celebrity
profiles if they have a queer and local angle, coverage of racial
minority issues that have a queer and local angle, Lesbian news
and views that have a queer and local angle
What is the best advice for someone contemplating writing for your publication? Send
in $3 and get the most current issue so you can see the quality of
writing and the types of columns and articles we're interested in.

Baltimore Gay Paper

241 W. Chase Street, Baltimore MD 21201
or   P.O. Box 2351 Baltimore MD 21203-4575
Regularity of Publication: Biweekly
Tel: 410 837 7748   Fax   410 837 8512
E-mail address: editor@bgp.org   website address: www.bgp.org
Editor: Daniel D'Arezzo
Advertising Manager: Lee Fister (410)-837-7748 or
                              e-mail to advertise@bgp.org

Baltimore Women's Times

PO Box 39773, Baltimore, MD 21212
Regularity of Publication: Monthly
Circulation: 400   Audited: No
Phone Number: 410/467-1605   E-mail address: ShirleyH1@aol.com
Advertising Manager: Shirley Hartwell 410/467-1605
Special needs of your publication: We run contests soliciting poetry,
essays, stories, articles; 1st prize is $50. Entries of any length are
considered.

MASSACHUSETTS

Bay Windows

631 Tremont Street, Boston, MA 02118
Regularity of Publication: Weekly
Circulation: 35,000   Audited: Yes
Phone Number: 617-266-6670   Fax Number: 617-266-5973
E-mail address: news@baywindows.com,
advertising@baywindows.com,   letters@baywindows.com
website address: www.baywindows.com
Publisher: James G. Hoover (ext. 214)
Editor: Jeff Epperly (ext. 217)
Managing Editor: Jeff Epperly (ext. 217)
Associate Editor: Peter Cassels (ext. 216)
Arts Editor: Rudy Kikel (ext. 211)
News Editor: Jeff Epperly (ext.217)
Advertising Manager: Sue O'Connell (ext. 215)
Average length of feature: 800-1,000 words
Minimum rate paid per word: payment varies according to length,
rights acquired. Minimum of $50 per article
Minimum rate paid for photos: $50
How do you prefer your stories to be filed? e-mail
How do you prefer to be contacted? e-mail
Special needs of your publication: Humor, Book Reviews, National news,
local news, Celebrity profiles, coverage of racial minority issues,
Lesbian news and views.
What is the best advice for someone contemplating writing for your publication?
Query first. Articles from non-regular and first-time contributors are
examined 'on spec.' We accept simultaneous submissions as long as
articles are not submitted to other publications in Boston market.

BiWomen

P.O. Box 639, Cambridge, MA 02140
Regularity of Publication: Bimonthly
Circulation: 400   Audited: No
Phone Number: 617-424-9595

116

E-mail address: eruthstr@mail.lesley.edu
Editor: Ellyn Ruthstrom 617-926-8737
Average length of feature: 500-1000 words
Minimum rate paid per word: no payment
Minimum rate paid for photos: no payment
How do you prefer your stories to be filed? email or on Mac disk
How do you prefer to be contacted? email
Special needs of your publication: We are the newsletter for the Boston
Bisexual Women's Network, though our readership is national and
some international as well. We have a feminist perspective; each
issue focuses on a theme and includes a two month calendar of the
Boston bi community. We accept photos, artwork appropriate for
one color printing, cartoons, reviews, features, and interviews.
What is the best advice for someone contemplating writing for your publication? Ask
for a sample copy and find out what the upcoming themes are.

The Guide: Gay Travel, Entertainment, Politics, and Sex

PO Box 990593, Boston, MA 02199
Regularity of Publication: monthly
Circulation: 30,000   Audited: no
Phone Number: (617) 266-8557   Fax Number: (617) 266-1125
E-mail address: theguide@guidemag.com
website address: www.guidemag.com
Publisher: Ed Hougen
Editor: French Wall
Features Editor: Bill Andriette
Average length of feature: 2500 words
Minimum rate paid per word: $.06-.15
Minimum rate paid for photos: $15
How do you prefer your stories to be filed? on disk
How do you prefer to be contacted? by email, or w/SASE
Special needs of your publication: humor, sex politics, scepticism of
pronoucements of spokespeople
What is the best advice for someone contemplating writing for your publication?
brevity and humor always appreciated; aspire to something loftier
than becoming a junior strait person

In Newsweekly

544 Tremont Street, Boston, MA 02116
Regularity of Publication: Weekly
Circulation: 20,000   Verified Audit pending
Phone Number: 617-426-8246   Fax Number: 617-426-8264
E-mail address: innews@aol.com
website address: www.innewsweekly.com
Publisher: Chris Robinson (ext. 301)
Editor: Rick Dunn (ext. 304)
                       editor@innewsweekly.com
News Editor: Fred Kuhr (ext. 311) fkuhr@aol.com
Advertising Manager: Chris Robinson (ext. 301)

LESBIAN CALENDAR

351 Pleasant Street #132, Northampton MA 01060
Phone 413 586 5514   E-mail: info@inetcon.com
Monthly

One in Ten

One in Ten, The Boston Phoenix, 126 Brookline Ave., Boston, MA 02215
Regularity of Publication: Monthly
Circulation: 100,000   Audited:Yes
Phone Number: (617) 859-3237   Fax Number: (617) 859-8201
E-mail address: homo@phx.com
website address: www.bostonphoenix.com
Editor: Susan Ryan-Vollmar
Average length of feature: 1500 words
Minimum rate paid per word: approx $250 per article
How do you prefer your stories to be filed? e-mail
How do you prefer to be contacted? e-mail
What is the best advice for someone contemplating writing for your publication? send clips of previously published work with 2 or 3 ideas. Please familiarize yourself with the publication before pitching the editor!!!!

118

MICHIGAN

Between The Lines

20793 Farmington Road #25, Farmington, MI 48336
Regularity of Publication: weekly
Circulation: 20,000   Audited: No
Phone Number: 248 615 7003   Fax Number: 248 615 7018
E-mail address: PridePBlis@aol.com
website address: www.Pridesource.com
Publishers   Jan Stevenson And Susan Horowitz
Editor in Chief   Susan Horowitz (ext. 30)
Advertising Manager: Jan Stevenson 888- 615 7003
Managing Editor: Cheryl Zupan (ext. 25)
Average length of feature: 1000 words
Minimum rate paid per word: 5 cents
Minimum rate paid for photos: $10
How do you prefer your stories to be filed? e-mail
How do you prefer to be contacted? e-mail

Kick Magazine

Box 2222, Detroit, MI 48231
Regularity of Publication: Monthly - 10 times-a-year
(double issues Dec/Jan, July/Aug)
Phone Number: 313-438-0704   Fax Number: 313-340-0076
E-mail address: kickpuco@aol.com
website address: www.kick-online.com
Publisher: Curtis Lipscomb lipscomb@kick-online.com
Editor: Jack Gorro
Managing Editor: Jason Michael
Average length of feature: 750-1000
Minimum rate paid per word: flat rate $25/feature
How do you prefer your stories to be filed? electronically in Word or as
text file
How do you prefer to be contacted? for submission inquiries, please contact
our managing editor directly at soulbro13@aol.com, for all other
business concerns, please contact our publisher at

kickpuco@aol.com
What is the best advice for someone contemplating writing for your publication? Keep in mind that we're designed for the mind, body and spirit of the black glbt community. We need features that will be enlightening and entertaining to them.

METRA MAGAZINE

PO Box 71844, Madison Heights, MI 48071
Regularity of Publication: BI MONTHLY
Circulation: 20,000   Audited: NO
Phone Number: 248-543-3500   Fax Number: 248-543-2810
E-mail address: METRAMAG@AOL.COM
website address: http//members.aol.com/metramag/index.html
Publisher: Mari Sappington (ext. 2)
Editor: (ext.3)
Arts Editor: (ext.3)
Advertising Manager: (ext. 1)

Out Post

P.O. Box 7117, Ann Arbor, MI 48107
Regularity of Publication: Biweekly
Circulation: 15,000
Phone Number: 313-702-0272   Fax Number: 734-332-8616
E-mail address: OPost@aol.com
Publisher: Steve Culver
Average length of feature:750 words
Minimum rate paid per word: 5¢
Minimum rate paid for photos: $5
How do you prefer your stories to be filed? Quickly (e-mail)
How do you prefer to be contacted? via USPS
Special needs of your publication: Cartoons, Humor, Celebrity profiles
What is the best advice for someone contemplating writing for your publication? Don't quit your day job

The Third Coast Magazine

PO Box 7296, Grand Rapids, Michigan, 49510.
E-mail: info@3rd-coast.net.

In March of 1995 Sara Mahan and Gary VanHarn published the first issue of The Third Coast Magazine. Inspired by friends to begin publication of a gay magazine, Sara and Gary ventured out to provide the gay community with a publication which offered personal stories, articles relating to gay issues, and current information about the gay community. From the first issue, Third Coast found its own niche among gay publications in Michigan. Readers responded favorably to the honest, challenging, and affirming nature of the magazine. Sara and Gary continued to publish the magazine through March of 1998 when the magazine was purchased by Franklin Van Pelt and Paul Snyder, a gay couple living in Grand Rapids, Michigan.

Van Pelt and Snyder, who had both been involved in Third Coast as writers, built on a the solid foundation laid by Mahan and VanHarn. Beginning with the April, 1998 issue, The Third Coast Magazine received a facelift and began distribution in a much wider area. The addition of color and an increase in size and number of pages provided additional room for more advertisers, and therefore, more monthly articles. Additional articles exploring lesbian, bisexual, and transgender issues as well as gay male issues helped round out the content of the magazine.

Third Coast Magazine is now distributed to gay owned or friendly bars, books stores, coffee houses, restaurants and other businesses in over twenty cities in Michigan, Ohio, and Indiana. The magazine is also mailed to major universities, gay and lesbian support groups, and AIDS treatment centers. Many individuals have subscribed to Third Coast to take advantage of the convenience of having the magazine mailed to their homes each month.

Publisher Franklin Van Pelt and Editor in Chief Paul H. Snyder are sincere in their main goal to be sure Third Coast lives up to it's motto - "Supporting and Celebrating the Lesbian, Gay, Bisexual, and Transgender Communities of the Great Lakes. To meet that goal, Plans are in process to reach out to additional cities around the Great Lakes. Contributions are welcome.

What Helen Heard

PO Box 811, East Lansing, MI 48826-0811
Regularity of Publication: bimonthly
Circulation: 5,000   Audited: No
Phone Number: 517 371 5257   Fax Number: 517 371 5200
E-mail address: elsiepub@aol.com
How do you prefer your stories to be filed? mail
How do you prefer to be contacted? mail
Special needs of your publication: cartoons, book reviews, national news, racial minority issues, lesbian news and views, for Michigan lesbians, statewide news, services and advertisers

WRAP-Up

Washtenaw Rainbow Action Project,
P.O. Box 7951, Ann Arbor, MI 48107
Regularity of Publication: Monthly
Circulation: Approx. 500   Audited: No
Phone Number: (734) 995-9867
E-mail address: wrap.aa@umich.edu
website address: http://comnet.org/wrap/
Editors: Jean Borger borger@umich.edu
                       Amanda Watson alwatson@umich.edu
Advertising Manager: Mark Leonard markleon@cris.com
Average length of feature: 300-800 words
Minimum rate paid per word: None
Minimum rate paid for photos: None
How do you prefer your stories to be filed? Via e-mail
How do you prefer to be contacted? Via e-mail
Special needs of your publication: Usually news is local and WRAP-based, since the publication is a newsletter. At times we cover state and national issues. Readership is the LGBT (and allies) community of Washtenaw County in southeastern Michigan.
What is the best advice for someone contemplating writing for your publication?
Contact the editors with a query before submitting.

MINNESOTA

Focus Point

401 N 3rd St. Suite 480, Minneapolis, MN 55401
Regularity of Publication: Weekly
Phone Number: 612-288-9008   Fax Number: 612-288-9001
E-mail address: focuspoint@qnexus.com
Publisher and Editor: C.A. Lindahl-Urben

Lavender

2344 Nicollet Ave. S., Suite 300, Minneapolis, MN 55404
Regularity of Publication: Biweekly
Circulation: 25,173   Audited: Yes
Phone Number: 612-871-2237   Fax Number: 612-871-2650
E-mail address: info@lavendermagazine.com
website address: lavendermagazine.com
Publisher: Lavender Lifestyles Marketing, Inc.
Editor: Rudy Renaud
Associate Editor: Jeremy Norton
Editorial Assistant: Sarah Petersen
Average length of feature: 700 words
Minimum rate paid for photos: $25
How do you prefer your stories to be filed? by e-mail
How do you prefer to be contacted? by e-mail
Special needs of your publication: Sports, racial minority issues, local news, quality color photos
What is the best advice for someone contemplating writing for your publication? e-mail rudy (rudy@lavendermagazine.com) an article for publication along with a cover letter. No phone calls! Lavender prefers local writers.

Siren:

An Information Source for Gay, Lesbian, Bisexual and Transgender People.

14th Avenue South #3, Minneapolis, MN 55407
Phone number: 612-676-2178
Regularity of Publication: Biweekly
Circulation: 40,000
Email address: sirenmedia@hotmail.com
Contacts: Susan Raffo, Donn Poll
Average length of feature: 1,200 words
Minute pay rate: contact us for rates
How do you prefer your stories to be filed: email
How do you prefer to be contacted: email
Specific needs of your publication: Book reviews, National news, Local news, Coverage of all parts of the gay, lesbian, bisexual and transgender community, essay and commentary work, investigative work, web-based services.
What is the best advice for someone contemplating writing for your publication? Pick up a copy and get to know us.

UPmagazine

1043 Grand Ave #322, St. Paul, MN 55105
Regularity of Publication: Monthly
Circulation: 20,000
Phone Number: 612.822.8335   Fax Number: 651.293.0313
E-mail address: info@upmagazine.com
website address: www.upmagazine.com
Editor: Tim Yoon
Online Editor: Cameron L. Cegelski
Production: John Hamer
Director of Operations: Micheal Karpowicz
Concerning Advertising Contact: Tim Yoon
Average length of feature: 500 words
How do you prefer your stories to be filed? email
How do you prefer to be contacted? email
Special needs of your publication: We're always seeking Women Contributors
What is the best advice for someone contemplating writing for your publication? Be a self starter and have a winning attitude.

MISSOURI

Current News

809-813 West 39th Street, Kansas City, MO 64111
Regularity of Publication: Weekly (Wed)
Circulation: 36,000   Audited: Yes
Phone Number: 816-753-4300   Fax Number: 816-753-2700
E-mail address: GetCurrent@aol.com
website address: www.currentnews.com
Publisher: GreyMatters
Managing Editor: J.D. O'Neal, II ext. 13)
Features Editor: Chuck Takett (ext. 21)
Arts Editor: Victer Hewer (ext. 18)
News Editor: Kevin Gertin (ext. 14)
Advertising Manager: Patti Johnson (ext. 16)
Average length of feature: 850-875 words
Minimum rate paid per word: Negotiable
Minimum rate paid for photos: Negotiable
How do you prefer your stories to be filed? Via Email
How do you prefer to be contacted? Via Email

EXPMagazine

4579 Laclede #110, St Louis, MO 63108-2103
Phone 314 367 0397   Fax: 314 727 1884
E-mail: Expmag@aol.com
bi-weekly

News-Telegraph

PO Box 14229-A, St. Louis, MO 63178 (main office),
PO Box 10085, Kansas City, MO 64171 (branch office)
we are the main news publication (as versus entertainment) for
both cities.
Regularity of Publication: twice a month (not every two weeks)
Circulation: 14,000   Audited: No

Phone Number(s): 314/664-6411 (SL) or 816/561-6266 (KC)
Fax Number(s): 314/664-6303 (SL) or 816/561-6266 (KC)
E-mail address: NTSTL@aol.com
Publisher: Piasa Publishing Co. 314/664-6411
Managing Editor: Jim Thomas
Advertising Manager: Jim Thomas
Average length of feature: 750-1500 words
Minimum rate paid per word: paid by article, negotiated
Minimum rate paid for photos: paid by photo, negotiated
How do you prefer your stories to be filed? e-mail
How do you prefer to be contacted? e-mail or phone
What is the best advice for someone contemplating writing for your publication? We favor stories which connect with our geographic region above those that don't, although we use both. Stories must have direct connection to Lesbian/Gay subject matter.

MONTANA

OutSpoken

P.O. BOX 7105, Missoula, MT. 59807-7105
Publisher: Cat Carrel
Email: OutspknMT@aol.com
Website: http://members.aol.com/outs pkn123
Special needs: Our goal is to create a sense of community within the gay/lesbian community of Montana. If you are at all interested, please drop us a line! We have over 60 drop off points around Missoula and the state. We publish the first of each month!

NEVADA

The Bugle

PO Box 14580, Las Vegas, NV 89114-4580
Phone number: 702-369-6260   Fax number: 702-369-9325
E-mail: LVBugle1@aol.com

Publisher: Brett McFarlane
Twice a month

Reno Informer Gay & Lesbian News

P.O. Box 33337, Reno, NV 89533
Circulation: 5000   Audited: No
Phone Number: 775-747-8833   Fax Number: 775-747-8833
E-mail address: reno-informer@earthling.net
website address: http://users.yellowsub.net/reno-informer/index.htm
Publisher and Editor: Eddie Ortiz
Advertising Manager: Vacant
Average length of feature: 500 words
Minimum rate paid per word: negotiable
Minimum rate paid for photos: negotiable
How do you prefer your stories to be filed? Email
How do you prefer to be contacted? U.S. Mail
Special needs of your publication: Cartoons, Book Reviews, National
news, local news, celebrity profiles, Lesbian news and views,
web-based services

NEW JERSEY

OUR QUARTERLY

PO Box 2201, Bloomfield, NJ 07003
Regularity of Publication: Bi-Monthly
Circulation: 10,000   Audited: No
Phone Number: 973 893 0455 Ext 7   Fax Number: 973 893 1370
E-mail address: OQEditor@aol.com
website address: www.ourquarterly.com
Publisher: Angela S. Calzone (ext. 1)
Editor: Debbie Mernoli (ext.2)
Advertising Manager: Debbie Mernoli (ext. 2)
Average length of feature: 1500-1700 words
Minimum rate paid per word: Most are not paid - compensated by
ad space
How do you prefer your stories to be filed? e-mail or fax

NEW MEXICO

Out! magazine

P.O. Box 27237, Albuquerque, NM 87125-7237
Regularity of Publication: Monthly
Circulation: 7,000   Audited: No
Phone Number: (505) 243-2540 (leave a message)
Fax Number: (505) 842-5114
E-mail address: mail@outmagazine.com
website address: www.outmagazine.com
Editor: Roy Reini (ext. 310)
                        editor@outmagazine.com
Advertising Manager: Steve Benoit (505) 245-7838 voice,
                        (505) 245-6655 fax
Average length of feature: 1500 words
Minimum rate paid per word: Pay by the article
Minimum rate paid for photos: Negotiated with photographer
How do you prefer your stories to be filed? via e-mail
How do you prefer to be contacted? either e-mail or fax
What is the best advice for someone contemplating writing for your publication?
Send samples, expected price of articles, and contact number. Out!
Magazine is created by a handful of people in our spare time. Please
allow a little time to process your correspondence.

NEW YORK

CommUnity

PO Box 131, Albany, NY 12201-0131
Regularity of Publication: Monthly
Circulation: 2,000 approx.   Audited: No
Phone Number: 518 462 6138 x37   Fax Number: 518 462 2101
E-mail address: cdglcc@aol.com   website: www.cdglcc.org
Editor: Susan Murphy (ext. 82)
How do you prefer to be contacted? fax or phone

128

Special needs of your publication: we cover a myriad of topics.
What is the best advice for someone contemplating writing for your publication?
please submit for consideration

Gayzette

PO Box 122, Utica, NY 13503-0122
Regularity of Publication: Monthly
Circulation: 800   Audited: No
Phone Number: 315-894-3565   E-mail address: timditty@aol.com
website address: http://members.aol.com/timditty/gulf.html
Publisher: GULF - Greater Utica Lambda Fellowship, Inc.
Editor: Tim Dittfield 315-894-3565
Advertising Manager: RJ Middlemiss
Average length of feature: varies
Minimum rate paid per word: 0
Minimum rate paid for photos: 0
How do you prefer your stories to be filed? on time
How do you prefer to be contacted? e-mail
Special needs of your publication: Local News
What is the best advice for someone contemplating writing for your publication?
Know the local area

Greenwich Village Gazette

245 East 11th St, NYC, NY 10003
or
P.O. Box 1023, Island Heights, NJ 08732
Regularity of Publication Weekly:
Circulation: 10,000   Audited: Yes
Phone Number: 1-800-670-3898
E-mail address: editor@gvny.com or editor@new1.com
website address: http://www.gvny.com or http://www.nycny.com
Editor: Richard Schiff 1-800-670-3898
Managing Editor: Nick Mamatas
Features Editor: Mary Barnet
Arts Editor: Joe Basta
Advertising Manager: Howard Flysher 1-202-461-8807
Average length of feature: 3000 words
Minimum rate paid per word: Contributions only at this time

Minimum rate paid for photos: Contributions only at this time
How do you prefer your stories to be filed?e-mail as .rtf or .doc files
How do you prefer to be contacted? e-mail
Special needs of your publication: All subjects are of interest
What is the best advice for someone contemplating writing for your publication? We
are an alternative weekly paper that is dead set to present the fairest
view of all matter relative to life today. We maintain that all people
are created equal and no less is acceptable. Go read it, and see if
you belong to that ilk of activistism.

HX Magazine

230 W 17th Street, 8th Floor, New York, NY 10011
Regularity of Publication: Weekly
Circulation: 40,000   Audited: Yes
Phone Number: 212-352-3535   Fax Number: 212-352-3596
E-mail address: hx@hx.com   website address: www.hx.com
Publisher: Matthew Bank
Editor: Bill Henning   editor@hx.com
Advertising Director: Gary Lacinski
Special needs of your publication that freelance writers might be able to fulfill: We
write almost all of our stories in-house, and use very few freelancers.
We don't pay by the word for assignments, we pay negotiated rates
that range from $25 to $100 per assignment. We should be contact-
ed by mail.

LGNY

150 Fifth Avenue 6th Floor, NY, NY 10011
Circulation: 35,000   Audited: Yes
Phone Number: 212-691-1100   Fax Number: 212-691-6185
E-mail address: lgny@nycnet.com
website address: http://www.lgny.com
Publisher: Troy Masters (ext. 21)
Editor: Paul Schindler (ext. 11)
Managing Editor: Seth Bookey   (ext. 12)
Features Editor: Duncan Osborne (ext. 11)
News Editor: Duncan Osborne
Advertising Manager: Daniel Bort
Average length of feature: 1800 words

130

Minimum rate paid per word: no per word payment/terms negotiated with writer
Minimum rate paid for photos: writer responsible for art/photo selection
How do you prefer your stories to be filed? query via email
How do you prefer to be contacted? email
Special needs of your publication: We are primarily a local news and social issues newspaper, but do features based on a wide variety of interests
What is the best advice for someone contemplating writing for your publication? Anyone can contribute if the ideas are insightful, forward thinking and raise new, fresh ideas. We are gay-owned and operated and are an independent publication. LGNY is interested in journalistic vibrancy and doesn't shy away from taking a position on issues or choosing not to report on a controversy in an attempt to "stay out of it."

METROSOURCE

180 Varick Street 5th Floor, New York, NY 10014
Regularity of Publication: Quarterly
Circulation: 85,000   Audited: Yes
Phone Number: 212 691 5127   Fax Number: 212 741 2978
E-mail address: metrosourc@aol.com
Publisher: Rob Davis
Editor: Eva Leonard
Advertising Manager: Jay Adams
Average length of feature: 1500 words
Minimum rate paid per word: Negotiable
Minimum rate paid for photos: Negotiable
How do you prefer your stories to be filed? E-mail
How do you prefer to be contacted? E-mail
Special needs of your publication: Need experienced freelance arts, food, travel, health and feature writers.
What is the best advice for someone contemplating writing for your publication? E-mail Eva Leonard.

NEW YORK BLADE NEWS

242 West 30th Street, 4th Floor, New York, NY 10001
Regularity of Publication : weekly
Circulation: We've retained audit circulation to prepare for our first audit. We began publishing in October 1997.

Phone Number: 212 268-2701   Fax Number: 212 268-2069
E-mail address: jlamont@nyblade.com
website address: www.nyblade.com
Publisher: Don Michaels
Assistant Publisher: James Lamont
Senior Editor: Lisa Keen
Arts Editor: Wayne Hoffman
News Editor: Mark Sullivan
Advertising Manager: James Lamont
Special needs of your publication: we are the weekly publication of New York City's gay and lesbian community.
What is the best advice for someone contemplating writing for your publication? Please send writing samples.

NEXT

121 Varick Street 6th Floor, New York, NY 10013
Phone: 212 627 0165   Fax: 212 627 0633
e-mail   nextmagazi@aol.com
Publisher: David Moyal
Editor: Jay Jimenez

Outcome

23 Lafayette Square # 226, Buffalo, NY 14203
Regularity of Publication: Monthly
Circulation: 5,000   `Audited: No
Phone Number: 716 441-7485/ 716 883-2756
E-mail address: Outcomewny@aol.com outcome-ed@juno.com
Publisher: Tim Moran (Buffalo Creek Media)
Editor: Tom Dooney qnewsed@juno.com
Advertising Manager: Tim Moran
Average length of feature: 1000 words
Minimum rate paid per word: negotiable
Minimum rate paid for photos: negotiable
How do you prefer your stories to be filed? email
How do you prefer to be contacted? email/phone
Special needs of your publication: Issue feature, National news, local news, coverage of racial minority issues, Lesbian news and views, web-based services

OUTLOOK - Long Island

P.O. Box 312, Brightwaters, NY 11718-0312
Regularity of Publication: Bi-Monthly
Circulation: 10,000   Audited: No
Phone Number: 516-968-7780   Fax Number: 516-206-1820
E-mail address: OutlookLI@aol.com
Publisher: Tom Hroncich   516-968-7780
Average length of feature: 500 words
How do you prefer to be contacted? E-mail
What is the best advice for someone contemplating writing for your publication? As
of the time of this submission, OUTLOOK - Long Island is still one
month away from our first issue being published. So my advice is
really more of a request: please bear with us as we get the magazine off the ground in the next several months and soon we will
know more about what sort of help we really need!

TWIST

73-34 70th Street, Glendale, NY 11385
or
P.O. Box 7908, Rego Park, NY 11374
Monthly
Phone Number: 718 381 8776   Fax Number: 718 366 8636
E-mail address: Twistmag@aol.com
Publisher: J.R. Valdes
Editors :   J.R. Valdes
Managing Editor: Steve Foster
Features Editor   Chris Johnson
Arts Editor   J.R. Valdes
News Editor   Eric Gregg
Adertising Manager: Steve Foster
How do you prefer stories to be filed: Quark

Voices Magazine

206 South Elmwood Avenue, Buffalo, NY 14201
Regularity of Publication: Monthly

Circulation: 4,000   Audited: No
Phone Number: 716 847 0315   Fax Number: 716 847 0418
E-mail address: VOICESMAG@ACSWNY.COM
Publisher: Matthew   John Pasquarella 716 847 0212 (ext. 368)
Editor: Brian Lampkin716 847 0315 (ext. 330)
Advertising Manager: Finley Cooperwood 716 847 0315 (ext. 335)
Average length of feature: 1500 words
Minimum rate paid per word: 0
Minimum rate paid for photos:0
How do you prefer your stories to be filed? Paper&E-mail/disk
Special needs of your publication: HIV/AIDS related, human sexuality contained
What is the best advice for someone contemplating writing for your publication?
Talk to the editor.

NORTH CAROLINA

Carolina Lesbian News

P.O. Box 8190, Charlotte, NC 28203
Phone: 704 559 5991   Fax: 704 333 9316
e-mail CLesbianN@aol.com

Community Connections

PO BOX 18088, Asheville, NC 28801
Regularity of Publication : Monthly
Circulation: 7500   Audited: No
Phone Number: 828-251-2449   Fax Number: 828-251-9880
E-mail address: lmorphew@buncombe.main.nc.us
Publisher and Managing Editor: Lisa Morphew 828-251-2449
Arts Editor: Carolyn Ogburn 828-251-2449
Advertising Manager: Lisa Morphew 828-251-2449
Average length of feature: 350-600 words
How do you prefer your stories to be filed? email or fax
How do you prefer to be contacted? phone/fax/email
Special needs of your publication that freelance writers might be able to fulfill:
Humor, Features, Horoscopes
What is the best advice for someone contemplating writing for your publication? We

134

are a non-profit community paper in business for 11 years. We like to publish portfolios of photographers work and special interest stories that we can get for free. We accept music reviews.

Down East Voice

PO Box 1691, Greenville, NC 27835-1691
Phone: (252) 551-0316   e-mail: beachpix@coastalnet.com
Publisher: Down East Pride

The Front Page

PO Box 27928, Raleigh, NC 27611
Regularity of Publication: Biweekly
Audited: No
Phone Number: 919 829 0181   Fax: 919 829 0830
E-mail address: frntpage@aol.com
Publisher and Senior Editor: Jim Baxter
Associate Editor and Business Manager: Jim Duley
Advertising Manager: Paul Falduto (919) 829 0181
Regularity of Publication: Biweekly
Average length of feature: 1,000-1,200 words
Minimum rate paid per word: 5-6 cents a word
Minimum rate paid for photos: $25
How do you prefer your stories to be filed? e-mail/disk only
How do you prefer to be contacted? e-mail/fax
What is the best advice for someone contemplating writing for your publication? Do not query- just e-mail it. We'll call you if we want to buy it.

Q-Notes

PO Box 221841, Charlotte, NC 28222
Regularity of Publication: Biweekly
Circulation: 10,000   Audited: No
Phone Number: (704) 531-9988   Fax Number: (704) 531-1838
E-mail address: Editorial: editor@q-notes.com
Ads: advertising@q-notes.com   website address: www.q-notes.com
Publisher: Jim Yarbrough publisher@q-notes.com
Editor: David Stout

Advertising Manager: Brian Myer
Average length of feature: 750 words
Minimum rate paid per word: 4 cents per word
How do you prefer your stories to be filed? E-mail
How do you prefer to be contacted? E-mail

Triangle Rag

PO Box 21156, Durham, NC 27703
Regularity of Publication: Bi-Monthly
Circulation: 5000   Audited: No
Phone Number: 919-680-3080   Fax Number: 919-680-3080
E-mail address: t-rag@gurlmail.com
Publisher: Leslie Cunningham
Editors: Sand Freeman/Lisa Franklin
How do you prefer to be contacted? via phone or email
Special needs of your publication: for lesbians and bisexual Women of color
in southern states. National feature articles, poetry, stories, erotica,
women's basketball, book club, film and music review, classified,
personals, community 411. All women of color national encouraged
to submit and input original writings.

OHIO

EXPOSE MAGAZINE

PO Box 26213, Akron, OH 44319
Regularity of Publication: Biweekly
Circulation: 3500
Phone Number:1-800-699-6131   Fax Number:330-830-6346
E-mail address: exposeusa@earthlink.net
website address: exposemag.com
main office: 330-830-8678 or toll free 800-699-6131
How do you prefer to be contacted? call the main office before mailing or
emailing any article.
Special needs of your publication:
Humor, national news, lesbian news and views.
What is the best advice for someone contemplating writing for your publication? Not

more than 800 words per article. We are a bar advertisment publication, we use articles for diversity, always looking for new talent. In the
case of our publication funny is better.

Gay People's Chronicle

P.O. Box 5426, Cleveland, OH 44101
For UPS, FedEx, and all other deliveries:
3121 Bridge Ave., Cleveland, Ohio 44113
Regularity of Publication: Weekly
Circulation: 18,000   Audited: No
Phone Number: 216-631-8646 or 800-426-5947
Fax Number: 216-631-1052
E-mail address: chronicle@chronohio.com
website address: www.cleveland.com/community/gay
Publisher: Martha Pontoni (ext. 31)
Managing Editor: vacant
Associate Editor   Brian DeWitt (ext. 13)
Advertising Manager: David Ebbert (ext. 19)
Average length of feature: 500-800 words
Minimum rate paid per word: speak with Managing Editor
Minimum rate paid for photos: $6
How do you prefer your stories to be filed? Via email to:
chronicle@chronohio.com
How do you prefer to be contacted? Via email
What is the best advice for someone contemplating writing for your publication?
Follow through on assignments, reliability, dependability, etc.

Outlook

The Independent Newspaper of the Greater Columbus Gay, Lesbian
and BisexualCommunity since 1996

700 Ackerman Road, Suite 600, Columbus, OH 43202
Regularity of Publication: biweekly (every other Thursday)
Circulation: 10,000 copies   Audited: Yes (The Media Audit)
Phone Number: (614)268-8525   Fax Number: (614) 261-8200
E-mail address: editor@outlooknews.com
website address: www.outlooknews.com
Publishers: C. Malcolm Riggle,
                           Lynn Greer and Jose Rodriguez

Editor: Lisa K. Zellner
Advertising Manager: contact the editor for advertising rates
Design and Art Director: Dan Crowe
We are restarting the publication after an ownership transition and
do not have a budget for freelance. Contributing writers are currently
volunteering their services.
How do you prefer to be contacted? email

The SPECTRUM

(incorporating The Catalyst)

5765 Philadelphia Dr. Dayton, OH 45415
Regularity of Publication: Monthly (1st Sat)
Circulation:5000   Audited: No
Phone Number(s):937-278-5482 or 1-888-422-0320 ext 7732
Fax Number(s):937-278-5877 or 1-888-422-0320 ext 7732.
E-mail address: Dspectrum@aol.com
website address: www.spectrumnews.com
Publisher and publisher: Lee Strausberg R.N. Main number
                             LeeRN937@aol.com
Assistant Editor: Dennis Given
Advertising Manager: Eddie Secrist   513-921-0240
                             or fax number above.
How do you prefer your stories to be filed? as an attached file using .txt
How do you prefer to be contacted? Email
Special needs of your publication: Deadline 20th of month preceding... We
are all volunteer! May consider others.
What is the best advice for someone contemplating writing for your publication? We
need help mostly with the local news and views.

Spotlight Magazine

P.O. Box 6339, Columbus, Ohio 43206
Regularity of Publication: Biweekly
Circulation: 2,000   Audited: No
Phone Number: (614) 253-6610
E-mail address: SpotlitMag@aol.com
website address: http://members.aol.com/spotlitmag
Publishers: Joseph Stefanko and Edwin John Yang
Managing Editor: Donna Welsh

Advertising Manager: Joseph Stefanko
Average length of feature: 800 words
Minimum rate paid per word: Negotiable
Minimum rate paid for photos: Negotiable
How do you prefer your stories to be filed? text file
How do you prefer to be contacted? e-mail, phone, or mail
Special needs of your publication that freelance writers might be able to fulfill:
humorous look at gay life, cartoons, soap opera style articles.
What is the best advice for someone contemplating writing for your publication? Have
fun with it.

Stonewall Journal

PO Box 10814, Columbus, OH 43201
UPS Delivery: 1160 N. High Street, Columbus, OH 43201
Regularity of Publication: Monthly
Circulation: 2500 in home mailings, 8000 printed   Audited: Yes
Phone Number: 614-299-7764   Fax Number: 614-299-4408
E-mail address: stnwall@ix.netcom.com
website address: www.stonewall-columbus.org
Publisher: Jeff Redfield, Stonewall Columbus
          Executive Director
Editor: Linda Thornburg
Advertising Manager: Tony Bellville
          Jay O'lack
Average length of feature: 500 – 1000 words
Minimum rate paid per word: pay per article
How do you prefer your stories to be filed? Text only format
How do you prefer to be contacted? Email or phone
Special needs of your publication: Predominately local news and news of
the organization, will feature some national news, especially if linked
to Columbus or parts of Ohio.
What is the best advice for someone contemplating writing for your publication?
Submit work to editor: usually only hire local people or people who
will donate their time (non-profit organization)

OKLAHOMA

The GAYLY OKLAHOMAN

Gayly Incorporated, P.O. Box 60930, Oklahoma City, OK 73146.
Publisher: Gayly Incorporated
Editor in Chief: Don Hawkins
Managing Editor: Jack Wozniak
Issue Editor: Don Hanks
Features Editor: Paula Brown
Out & About Editor: Victor Gorin/Delon Harris
Advertising Sales Manager: Jon Patterson:
                                405-528-0800/ 918-599-9380
Phone: 918-599-9380 (Tulsa); 405-528-0800 (OKC)
Fax: 405-528-0796   E. Mail: gaylyok@aol.com.
Issued on the 1st & 15th of each month
The Gayly Oklahoman is a bi-monthly news and events publication
targeted at the gay and lesbian communities of Oklahoma.

Tulsa Family News

PO Box 4140, Tulsa, OK 74159-0140
Phone 918 583 1248   Fax 918 583 4615
Publisher & Editor: Tom Neal
Issued on or before the 1st of each month

OREGON

Just Out

P.O. Box 14400, Portland OR, 97293-0400
Regularity of Publication: Biweekly on the first and third Friday or
each month
Phone Number: 503 236 1252   Fax Number: 503 236 1257
E-mail address: justout@justout.com

Publisher: Marty David
News Editor: Inga Sorenson   inga@justout.com
Entertainment Editor: Will O'Bryan
Advertising Director: Meg Grace 503 236 1253

Prizm

P.O. Box 927. Ashland. OR 97520   or
c/o Abdill-Ellis Lambda Community Center,
56 Third St., Ashland, OR 97520
Regularity of Publication: monthly
Phone Number: (541) 488-9107
E-mail address: lambdacntr@aol.com

Quotidian

formerly "The Ladies Social Register"

PO box 3214, Albany, OR 97321
Regularity of Publication: monthly
Circulation: 200   Audited: No
Phone Number: 541 928-0871
E-mail address: quotidian@proaxis.com
website address: wwwproaxis.com~quotidian
Publisher: Linda L. Klinge
Editor: SAA
Features Editor: Colleen Candee
Advertising Manager: L. Klinge
Average length of feature: two pages
Minimum rate paid per word: free copy of issue
How do you prefer to be contacted? email or snail mail
Special needs of your publication: : Cartoons, Humor, Book Reviews,
National news, local news, Celebrity profiles, coverage of racial
minority issues, Lesbian news and views.
What is the best advice for someone contemplating writing for your publication?
Contact us first.

PENNSYLVANIA

Au Courant

P.O. Box 42741, Philadelphia, PA 19101
or
2124 South Street, Philadelphia, PA 19146
Regularity of Publication: Weekly, Tuesdays
Circulation: 10,000   Audited: No
Phone Number: 215.790.1179   Fax Number: 215.790.9721
E-mail address: pridewk@pond.com
website address: www.au-courant.com (under construction at this time)
Publishers: Joseph Farrell/Colleen O'Connell 790.1179
Editor: Colleen O'Connell 790.1179
Advertising Manager: George Bullock 790.1179
Average length of feature: 700 words for feature, 1400 for cover
story, 300 art/book review
Minimum rate paid per word: $.10
Minimum rate paid for photos: $15.00
How do you prefer your stories to be filed? Email
How do you prefer to be contacted? email
Special needs of your publication: Coverage of arts and entertainment,
local and New York; Coverage of leather/fetish community; Analysis
and social commentary
What is the best advice for someone contemplating writing for your publication? Most
successful applicants have sent an idea for a story through email.
We tend to favor analysis and commentary over "news."

ERIE Gay News

"Covering News & Events in the Erie PA, Cleveland, Pittsburgh,
Buffalo & Chautauqua County NY Region"

1115 W 7th St, Erie, PA 16502-1105
Regularity of Publication: Monthly
Circulation: 2,000   Audited: No
Phone Number: (814) 456-9833   Fax Number: (814) 452-1392
E-mail address: info@eriegaynews.com
website address: http://www.eriegaynews.com

Publisher: All same: Michael Mahler & Micheal Miller (814) 456-9833 (it's our home)
Average length of feature: 250-500 words
Minimum rate paid per word: 0. We have no paid writers nor do we anticipate it
Minimum rate paid for photos: 0
How do you prefer your stories to be filed? Email
How do you prefer to be contacted? Email
Special needs of your publication: Predominantly local news and events.
What is the best advice for someone contemplating writing for your publication? We are usually only interested in local writers writing about local news and events. No paid staff at all.

Labyrinth (The Philadelphia Womens' Newspaper)

Westbury Publishing, Inc.
271 S. 15th St., Ste. 1706, P.O. Box 58489, Philadelphia, PA 19102
Phone: 215-546-6686   Fax: 215-546-1156
E-mail: mail@labyrinthnews.com
Advertising: ads@labyrinthnews.com
Published ten times a year

OUT

OUT Publishing Co. Inc
747 South Ave, Pittsburgh, PA 15203-2134
Regularity of Publication: Monthly
Circulation: 30,0000   Audited: No
Phone Number: 412 243 3350   Fax Number: 412 243 7989
E-mail address: Pghsout@aol.com
website address: www.outpub.com
Publisher: Tony Strejcek
Managing Editor: Jeff Howells
Features Editor: David Doorley
News Editor: Lisa Pasquini
Advertising Manager: Tony Strejcek
Average length of feature: 750-1500 words
Minimum rate paid: $25
Minimum rate paid for photos: $25

How do you prefer your stories to be filed? mail/e-mail/fax
How do you prefer to be contacted? mail/e-mail/fax
Special needs of your publication: Book Reviews, National news.
What is the best advice for someone contemplating writing for your publication? Send inquiry along with sample or column for publication.

The Philadelphia Gay News

505 South 4th Street, Philadelphia, PA 19147-1506
Phone Number: 215 625 8501   Fax Number: 215 925 6437
E-mail: pgn@epgn.com masco@aol.com
Website: http://www.epgn.com
Publisher: Mark Segal   mark@epgn.com
Editor   Patti Tihey tihey@epgn.com
Advertising Manager: Rick Lombardo rickl@epgn.com

Planet Q Newspaper

P.O. Box 81246, Pittsburgh, PA 15217
or
5421 Butler Street, Pittsburgh, PA 1520

Regularity of Publication: Monthly
Circulation: 12,000   Audited: No
Phone Number: 412-784-1500 or 412 855 5215
Fax Number: 412-784-1575
E-mail address: PlanetQ@aol.com
Publisher and Editor: Billy Hileman
Managing Editor: Andrew Greiner
Arts Editor: John Michael Curlovich
Advertising Manager: Billy Hileman until new hire
Average length of feature: 1000 words
Minimum rate paid per word: $0.05
Minimum rate paid for photos: $5
How do you prefer to be contacted? Email
Special needs of your publication: national news; book reviews, Lesbian local news is very important to us. Local and national news regarding feminist issues; choice; race relations and racism; transgender and bisexual issues; youth news and views

144

What is the best advice for someone contemplating writing for your publication? be thoughtful, challenging and accurate.

SPOTS

PO Box 99, Lake Ariel, PA 18436
Regularity of Publication: Monthly
Circulation: 5,000   Audited: No
Phone Number: 570-698-7725
E-mail address: spots@homohome.net
website address: http://www.homohome.net/spots/
Publisher: Louis Wolfe
Managing Editor: Sequinn
Features Editor: Michael Stewart
Arts Editor: Williams P. Hines
News Editor: Sequinn
Advertising Manager: Louis Wolfe
Average length of feature: 900 words
Minimum rate paid per word: Currently all work done in-house
Minimum rate paid for photos: Currently all work done in-house
How do you prefer your stories to be filed? e-mail with hard copy back-up mailed
How do you prefer to be contacted? e-mail with hard copy back-up mailed
Special needs of your publication that freelance writers might be able to fulfill: We currently are a newer and very local focused publication. Our market also receives copies of many of the surrounding major market weekly papers which fill the need for national news and many of the lifestyle pieces that fill the pages between advertisers.
What is the best advice for someone contemplating writing for your publication? Inquire if there is even a need for your materials.

PUERTO RICO

Puerto Rice Breeze

P.O. Box 16168, San Juan, PR 00908-6168
Telephone (787) 724 3411   E-Mail: ktoontz@rapidnetpr.net
Publisher/Editor: Tom Koontz

Co-Publisher: Eric Brahm
Spanish Editor/Translations: Iris Medina and Geraldine Bayron

RHODE ISLAND

OPTIONS Rhode Island's Lesbian & Gay Newspaper

PO Box 6406; Providence, RI 02940-6406
Regularity of Publication: Monthly (10 issues a year)
Circulation: 6000   Audited: No
Phone Number: 401 831-4519   Fax Number: 401 272-3247
E-mail address: gayoptions@aol.com or options@glbt.net
website address: www.GLBT.net/options
Publisher: OPTIONS Collective   Michael Guy
Editor: Gary Richards
Features Editor: Sally Ann Hay
News Editor   Brian Mulligan
Advertising Manager: Kate Katzberg
Length 1,500 words
Minimum Paid for Photos: $25
How do you prefer stories to be filed: e-mail
How do you prefer to contacted? e-mail/fax
Special needs of your publication: only local news; more volunteers, AIDS
Updates, Book reviews, Racial Minority Issues,
What is the best advice for someone contemplating writing for your publication?
We are all volunteer publication covering all aspects of glbt life in the
Rhode Island area. We are only interested in local writers, writing
about local issues and local stories.

SOUTH CAROLINA

In Unison

PO Box 8024, Columbia, SC 29202-8024
Phone: 803-771-0804   E-mail: NUnison@aol.com

146

TENNESSEE

Colors! Magazine

P.O. Box 50536, Nashville, TN 37205
Regularity of Publication: Monthly
Circulation: 3500   Audited: No
Phone Number: 615-356-8476   E-mail address: GoColors@aol.com
Publisher: Effie Hooha 615-356-8476
Editor: Mikhail Brown 615-356-8476
Average length of feature: 500 words
Minimum rate paid per word: negotiable
Minimum rate paid for photos: negotiable
How do you prefer your stories to be filed? e-mail
How do you prefer to be contacted? e-mail only
Special needs of your publication: Cartoons, Humor, local news
What is the best advice for someone contemplating writing for your publication?
Make it humorous, interesting, well-written and to the point!

Family & Friends

P O Box 771948, Memphis, TN 38177-1948
Regularity of Publication: Monthly
Circulation: 3,500   Audited: No
Phone Number: (901) 682-2669   Fax Number: (901) 685-2234
E-mail address: FamilyMag@aol.com
website address: http://members.aol.com/familymag/homepage.html
Editor: Anita Moyt (901) 682-2669
Advertising Manager: Anita Moyt (901) 682-2669
Average length of feature: 1200 words
Minimum rate paid for photos: $2.00
How do you prefer your stories to be filed? E-mail
How do you prefer to be contacted? Tel, fax or e-mail
Special needs of your publication: Humor, only local news, Celebrity profiles, Lesbian news and views
What is the best advice for someone contemplating writing for your publication? The shorter the better; we look for professionalism and unique angles.

Query, Tennessee's Lesbian and Gay Newsweekly

P.O. Box 24241, Nashville, TN 37202-4241
Regularity of Publication: Weekly
Circulation: 15,000   Audited: No
Phone Number: (615) 259-4135
E-mail address: QueryNews1@aol.com
Editor/Publisher: Jeffrey Ellis
Features Editor: Lynn Singer
Advertising Manager: Steve Wilson
Average length of feature: 750-1,000 words
Minimum rate paid per article: $25
Minimum rate paid for photos: $10
How do you prefer your stories to be filed? By email
How do you prefer to be contacted? By email, phone or query letter
Special needs of your publication: Personality features, news features
What is the best advice for someone contemplating writing for your publication? Be prepared with examples of your work

RFD

P.O. Box 68, Liberty, TN 37095
Regularity of Publication: Quarterly
Circulation: 3,000   Audited: No
Phone Number: 615 536 5176   E-mail address: mail@rfdmag.org
website address: www.redmag.org
Publisher: RFD Press
Business Manager: Gabby Haze 615 536 5176
Minimum rate paid per word: Paid with contributors copies
How do you prefer your stories to be filed? e-mail/e-mail attachment
How do you prefer to be contacted? e-mail

Triangle Journal News

P.O. Box 11485, Memphis, TN 3811-0485
Regularity of Publication: Monthly
Circulation: 400   Audited: No
Phone Number: 901-454-1411   Fax Number: 901-454-1411

E-mail address: memphistjn@aol.com
website address: www.memphistjn.com
Publisher and Editor: Allen Cook
Features and Arts Editor: Vincent Astor
Average length of feature: 500-800 words
Minimum rate paid per word: pay $25 per feature within above range
Minimum rate paid for photos: $10 per
How do you prefer your stories to be filed? doesn't matter e-mail, typed copy
How do you prefer to be contacted? Phone or email
What is the best advice for someone contemplating writing for your publication?
Knock yourself out! If you submit something ALWAYS (even if you
think I already have the address/phone #) include an easy way to
get back to you. Preference is always given to local material, but
there is usually room for much more.

Xenogeny

Your Mid-South Lesbigaytran News Weekly Serving Tennessee,
Kentucky, Alabama

P.O. Box, 1792, Antioch, Tennessee 37011
Regularity of Publication: Weekly
Circulation: 5,000   Audited: No
Phone Number: voice/fax: (615) 831-1806
Fax Number: voice/fax: (615) 831-1806
E-mail address: XenogenyX@aol.com
Publisher: Linda Welch
Editor: K.D. Adcock
Managing Editor: Michelle Renee
Advertising Manager: Del Dorr
Average length of feature: 850 words
Minimum rate paid for photos: varies
How do you prefer your stories to be filed? E-mail article in the body of an e-mail letter
How do you prefer to be contacted? Phone/e-mail
What is the best advice for someone contemplating writing for your publication? We
are a small publication with a big heart, but a small budget!

TEXAS

Central Texas Alliance News

Phone number: 254 715 6501   E-mail: GLACT111@aol.com
Regularity of Publication: Monthly
Publisher: Gay & Lesbian Alliance of Central Texas
Phone: 254 752 7727   800-735 1122   E-mail: stbail@aol.com

The Coastal Bend Community Press

1315 Craig St., Corpus Christi, TX 78404
Regularity of Publication: Bimonthly
Circulation: 5000
Phone Number: 361-776-4989   Fax Number: (630) 578-0995
E-mail address: cbcp@cbgpa.com
website address: www.cbgpa.com
Publisher: Coastal Bend Gay Pride Alliance
Editor in Chief: Andy Wilcox
Advertising Manager: Wendy Lee
How do you prefer your stories to be filed? E-mail
How do you prefer to be contacted? E-mail
What is the best advice for someone contemplating writing for your publication?
Coastal bend Community Press is the official publication of the
Coastal Bend Gay Pride Alliance and the only Gay publication in the
Coastal bend area of Texas. We are a nonprofit group with no funds.
All submissions will be considered for publication.

Dallas Voice

3000 Carlisle, Suite 200, Dallas, TX 75204
Regularity of Publication: Weekly (on Fridays)
Circulation: 15,000   Audited: No
Phone Number: 214-754-8710   Fax Number: 214-969-7271
E-mail address: editor@dallasvoice.com
website address: www.dallasvoice.com
Publisher: Robert Moore, ext. 112

Editor: Dennis Vercher, ext. 113
Lifestyles Editor (features/arts):   Daniel Kusner, ext. 118
Advertising Manager: Leo Cusimano, ext. 114
Average length of feature: 1200 words
Average length of spot news: 800 words
Minimum rate paid per word: No per word rate; fees are negotiated
based on estimated length and overall work required to produce the
feature (number of interviews, travel, etc.).
Minimum rate paid for photos: $10 per published photo.
How do you prefer your stories to be filed? By e-mail
How do you prefer to be contacted? By telephone or e-mail
Special needs of your publication: Op/ed columns, national celebrity inter-
views, features on gay and/or lesbian cultural topics.
What is the best advice for someone contemplating writing for your publication?
Call editor or lifestyles editor first.

The Houston Voice

500 Lovett Blvd., Ste. 200 Houston, TX 77006
Regularity of Publication: Weekly
Circulation: 11,500   Audited: No
Phone Number: 713-529-8490   Fax Number: 713-529-9531
E-mail address: feedback@houstonvoice.com
website address: www.houstonvoice.com
Associate Publisher: Mike Fleming - mike@houstonvoice.com
Editor: Anthony Connolly editor@houstonvoice.com
Advertising Manager: Mike Fleming
Average length of feature: 850 words
Minimum rate paid per word: varies
Minimum rate paid for photos: varies
How do you prefer your stories to be filed? Email
How do you prefer to be contacted? Email or Telephone

OutSmart Magazine

3406 Audubon Place, Houston, Texas 77006
Regularity of Publication: Monthly
Circulation: estimated readership 30,000   Audited: No
Phone Number: 713/520-7237   Fax Number: 713/522-3275
E-mail address: Letters@OutSmartMagazine.com

website address:	OutSmartMagazine.com
Publisher:	Greg Jeu (ext. 11)
Managing Editor:	Greg Jeu
	greg@outsmartmagazine.com (11)
Features Editor:	Melissa Valenzuela (ext. 22)
Arts Editor:	Blase DiStefano (ext. 17)
News Editor:	Melissa Valenzuela (ext. 22)
Advertising Manager:	Greg Jeu (ext. 11)

Average length of feature: 800-3600 words
Minimum rate paid per word: (pay per story)
Minimum rate paid for photos: (pay per photo)
How do you prefer your stories to be filed? Either send hardcopy by mail or send via internet
How do you prefer to be contacted? by letter or e-mail
What is the best advice for someone contemplating writing for your publication? Send for writers guidelines/ or obtain them on our website.

OUTspoken

P.O. Box 33561, Amarillo, Texas   79120-3561
Regularity of Publication: Monthly
Circulation: 200-300   Audited: No
Phone Number: (806) 356-9600   Fax Number: (806) 356-6624
E-mail address: FlyingPigs@aol.com
website address: www.users.arn.net/~jason808/outstanding
Editor: Kay C. Peck (806) 356-9600
Average length of feature: 200-300 words
Minimum rate paid per word: contributor's copies
Minimum rate paid for photos: only use locally generated photos
How do you prefer to be contacted? Via email BEFORE writing anything
Special needs of your publication: Local news and features only
What is the best advice for someone contemplating writing for your publication? Contact the editor first

TATS Newsletter

(...of the Texas Assn. for Transsexual Support)

TATS P O Box 142, Bellaire, TX 77401
Regularity of Publication: Monthly
Circulation: 125   Audited: No

Phone Number: 713-780-4282 (voice mail)
E-mail address: TATS@genderweb.org, MoonFlowrr@aol.com
Publisher and Editor: Vanessa Edwards Foster 281-584-9901
Advertising Manager: Vanessa Edwards Foster 281-584-9901
Average length of feature: 12 pages (unsure of count of words)
Minimum rate paid per word: Gratis
Minimum rate paid for photos: Gratis
How do you prefer to be contacted? Email
Special needs of your publication: Cartoons, Humor, Book reviews, National news, local news, Celebrity profiles, coverage of racial minority issues, Lesbian news and views
What is the best advice for someone contemplating writing for your publication?
We're a shoestring type organization dealing as a support function for transsexuals in the greater Houston area. Any articles of interest to trans-folk worldwide (including GLB issues that indirectly or directly affect us as well) are items we are interested in. Most articles are usually kept to about a page (9 pt. Times font), or roughly about 2000 words max. However we do take mucher shorter blurbs as well.

The Texas Triangle

4001-C, Cedar Springs, Dallas, TX 75219
Regularity of Publication: Weekly
Circulation: 25,000,   Verified Audit
Phone Number(s):   Dallas: 214-599-0155;
Austin: 512-476-0576;   Houston: 713-521-5822
Fax Number: 214-599-0156
E-mail address: txtriangle@aol.com
Publisher: Todd Cunningham 214-599-0155
Co-Editor, Dallas: Stephen R. Underwood 214-599-0155
Co-Editor, Houston: Nancy Ford, 713-521-5822
Advertising Manager: James Bengfort 214-599-0155
Average length of a news article: 750
Average length of an entertainment article: 750-1500
Average length of a cover story: 2000
Minimum rate paid per word: depends on content and exclusivity
Minimum rate paid for photos: depends on content and exclusivity
How do you prefer your stories to be filed? Email to anglemedia@aol.com
How do you prefer to be contacted? Call Dallas office.
What is the best advice for someone contemplating writing for your publication?

A gay Texas angle is an obvious plus. With a few exceptions, if a story is so generic it can run in Maine or Miami, we're probably not interested. We use the magazine format style for writing and the AP stylebook for punctuation. Our layout consists of news, opinion, a weekly cover story, and an entertainment section. Cover stories range from a variety of subjects, from leather to lesbians, but for the most part, we want them to be Texas based. It's a big state, and somebody's got to cover it. But since we distribute to over 500 locations statewide, any writer has almost limitless options.

This Week In Texas

500 Lovett Boulevard #102, Houston, TX 71006 (Houston)
3300 Reagan, Dallas, TX 75219 (Dallas Sales Office)
Regularity of Publication: Weekly
Circulation: 20,000   Audited: No
Phone Number(s):   713 527 9111   214 521 0622
Fax Number(s):   713 527 8948   214 520 8948
E-mail address: twtmag@aol.com
Publisher: Allen Gellman
Managing Editor: Richard Bang
Features/Arts/News Editor: Chris Salza
Advertising Manager: Steve Nally / Steve Miles (Dallas)
Average length of feature: 1,200 words
Minimum rate paid per story: $40-50
Minimum rate paid for photos: $10
How do you prefer your stories to be filed? E-mail
How do you prefer to be contacted? E-mail
Special needs of your publication: Think Texas, and Texas related
What is the best advice for someone contemplating writing for your publication?
This is a Texas based publication with a GLBT readership

The Transmission Line

(newsletter of the Gulf Coast Transgender Community)

GCTC,P O Box 66643, Houston, TX 78266-0643
Regularity of Publication: Monthly
Circulation: 100   Audited: No
Phone Number: 713-780-4282 (voice mail)

E-mail address: MCDesi@flash.net, MoonFlowrr@aol.com
Publisher: Silverheart Productions
Editor: Desirée Walton 713-807-1130
Managing Editor: Desirée Walton 713-807-1130
Features Editor: Vanessa Edwards Foster 281-584-9901
Advertising Manager: Desirée Walton   713-807-1130
                       Vanessa Edwards Foster   281-584-9901

Average length of feature: 8 pages   (unsure of count of words)
Minimum rate paid per word: Gratis
Minimum rate paid for photos: Gratis
How do you prefer to be contacted? Email
Special needs of your publication: Cartoons, Humor, Book reviews, National news, local news, Celebrity profiles, coverage of racial minority issues, Lesbian news and views.
What is the best advice for someone contemplating writing for your publication?
We're an open membership support group for transgenders of all ilks, budgeted very conservatively. Any articles of interest to trans-folk worldwide (including GLB issues that indirectly or directly affect us as well) are items we are interested in. Most articles are usually kept to about a page (9 pt. Times font), or roughly about 2000 words max. However we do take mucher shorter blurbs as well.

UTAH

The Pillar of the Gay and Lesbian Community

P.O. Box 57744, Salt Lake City, Utah 84157
Regularity of Publication: Monthly
Circulation: 6,000   Audited: No
Phone Number: (801) 265-0066   Fax Number: (801) 261-2923
E-mail address: PillarSLC@aol.com
website address: members@aol.com/PillarSLC
Publisher: Todd Dayley
Average length of feature: 1000 words
Minimum rate paid per word: Negotiable
Minimum rate paid for photos: Negotiable
How do you prefer your stories to be filed? e-mail text
How do you prefer to be contacted? e-mail

VERMONT

Out in the Mountains

PO Box 1078, Richmond, VT 05477-1078
Regularity of Publication: Monthly
Circulation: 6200   Audited: No
Phone Number: 802-434-6486   Fax Number: 802-434-7046
E-mail address: oitm@together.net
website address: www.vtpride.org
Managing Editor: Barbara Dozetos main number, no extention
Average length of feature: 1000 - 1200 words
Minimum rate paid per word: We are a volunteer publication. We
work hard to produce a final product that gives our writers quality
clips, however. We are very generous with copies for writers.
How do you prefer your stories to be filed? email
How do you prefer to be contacted? email
Special needs of your publication: we use almost entirely local writers or
stories with a specifically Vermont slant.
What is the best advice for someone contemplating writing for your publication?
Read a copy or two first - a recent copy. While we pride ourselves on
using local voices, a Vermont slant on a national issue might work.
Don't be fooled by the fact that we are non-profit and volunteer. We
do tight editing and produce a polished product. Most of all, don't
start your query with a greeting to an editor who left the paper 4
years ago.

VIRGINIA

Out & About In Virginia

P.O. Box 1414, Norfolk, VA 23501
Regularity of Publication:Monthly
Circulation: 12,000   Audited: No
Phone Number: 757-583-7468
E-mail address: vaoutabout@aol.com

156

Publisher and Editor: Henry Edgar
Advertising Manager: Henry Edgar
Average length of feature: 2-3 pages
Minimum rate paid per word: Negotiable
Minimum rate paid for photos: Negotiable
How do you prefer your stories to be filed? e-mail
How do you prefer to be contacted? e-mail/phone
Special needs of your publication: primarily local news. Always interested in more lesbian news. Somewhat celebrity interviews. National columns that have significance in Virginia
What is the best advice for someone contemplating writing for your publication? It must be skewed toward what people in Virginia are interested in. It should affect Virginia in one way or another. Our strength is local coverage; that's what our readers want. There are many places they can find national news; we're the only place they can find local news.

Shout!

P. O. Box 21201, Roanoke, VA 24018
Regularity of Publication: Monthly
Circulation: 8000   Audited: No
Phone Number: 540-989-1579   Fax Number: 540-989-1579
E-mail address: shoutzine@aol.com
website address: www.shoutmag.com
Publisher and Editor: Patrick McKinney 540-989-1579
Average length of feature: 1000 words
Minimum rate paid per word: currently no monetary compensation
How do you prefer your stories to be filed? e-mail
How do you prefer to be contacted? e-mail or snail mail
Special needs of your publication: Shout! is predominantly an entertainment and club paper that also covers local news

WASHINGTON

Capital "Q" News

5840 123rd Ave. SE, Tenino, WA 98589
Regularity of Publication: Monthly

Circulation: 3000   Audited No
Phone Number: 360.264.2545   E-mail address: OlyQnews@aol.com
Average length of feature: words 2500
Minimum rate paid per word: no pay
Minimum rate paid for photos: $5
Publisher: Alan Artas
Special needs of your publication: Deadline is the 15th of every month

Leather Pride

1122 E. Pike Street #707, Seattle, WA 98122-3934
e-mail: Lthrpride@aol.com   Website: http://home.aol.com/lthrpride
Serves Washington State and the Pacific North West leather community

Qink Magazine

PBM #1151, 1122 E Pike Street, Seattle, WA 98122
Regularity of Publication: Biweekly
Circulation:12,000 issues in 3 markets
(Seattle-WA, Portland-OR & Vancouver-BC,)
Audited: No
Phone Number: 206-419-7009   Fax Number: 206-374-2315
E-mail address: qinknw@aol.com
website address: http://members.aol.com/qinknw
Editor: Michael Gardunio
Average length of feature: 800 words
Minimum rate paid per word: $25 per column/Article flat rate
How do you prefer your stories to be filed? Via e-mail
How do you prefer to be contacted? Via e-mail
Special needs of your publication: Arts reviews, Book, Film and Music Reviews

Seattle Gay News

PO Box 22007, Seattle, WA 98122
Regularity of Publication: Weekly
Phone Number: 206 324 4297   Fax Number: 206 322 7188
E-mail address: sgn1@sgn.org
website address: www.sgn.org/sgn
Publisher: R. George Bakan rgbakan@aol.com

Editor: Tom Flint sgn3@sgn.org
Managing Editor: Matt Nagle
Advertising Manager: Bob Scofield
Average length of feature: 500 words
Minimum rate paid per word: negotiable
Minimum rate paid for photos: negotiable
How do you prefer your stories to be filed? mail
How do you prefer to be contacted? phone
What is the best advice for someone contemplating writing for your publication?
Speak to editors first...

Stonewall News Northwest (formal)

Stonewall or Stonewall News, even SNN (locally)

P.O. Box 3994, Spokane, WA 99220-3994
Regularity of Publication: Monthly
Circulation: 3,000 free and paid to Eastern Washington, the Idaho
Panhandle and Western Montana
Audit: No
Phone: (509) 456-8011   Fax: (509) 455-7013
E-Mail: SNNspokane@aol.com
Publisher and Editor: John M. Deen
Average Feature: 1,000 words
Rate per article: $25
How should stories be filed: e-mail
Contact: Call first
Special needs of your publication: National news and photos or art,
cartoons, puzzles, political cartoonist
Advice: Call first, then fax

WEST VIRGINIA

THRESHOLD MAGAZINE

1509 C Jackson Street, Charleston, WV 25311
Regularity of Publication: Monthly
Circulation: 1000   Audited: No
Phone Number: 304 926 8401

E-mail address: EarthMeadow@ivillage.com
or   LitlChaos@gurlmail.com
Publisher: T L Muncy and Yolanda Jackson 304 926 8401
All publication duties shared by Threshold's Publishers.
Average length of feature: 200-300 words
Minimum rate paid per word: Pays In copies
Minimum rate paid for photos: Pays in copies
How do you prefer your stories to be filed? via E-Mail or US Mail
How do you prefer to be contacted? Via E-Mail or US Mail
Special needs of your publication: Cartoons, humor, book reviews, national news,celebrity profiles, lesbian news and views, crossword submissions
We are also seeking submissions (viewpoints, news, photos, etc) from transplanted WV g/l/b/t contributors living in other states.
What is the best advice for someone contemplating writing for your publication? Be creative. Bring your own flavor to Threshold.

WISCONSIN

IN Step

1661 N. Water St., Suite 411, Milwaukee, WI 53202
Regularity of Publication: BiWeekly
Circulation: 15,000   Audited: Yes
Phone Number: 414.278.7840   Fax Number: 414.278.5868
E-mail address: instepnews@aol.com
website address: www.instepnews.com
Publisher and editor: William Attewell (ext. 3)
editor@instepnews.com
Features Editor: Ed Grover   edgrover@instepnews.com
Arts Editor: Jorge Cabal (ext.1)
jorgecabal@instepnews.com
Average length of feature: 1,000-1500 words
Minimum rate paid per word: Writers paid $15 to $75 per submission
Minimum rate paid for photos: $10
How do you prefer your stories to be filed? via e-mail
How do you prefer to be contacted? e-mail/us post
Special needs of your publication: Cartoons, Humor, Book Reviews, National news, local news, Celebrity profiles, coverage of racial

minority issues, Lesbian news and views

What is the best advice for someone contemplating writing for your publication?
Query first. Be professional. Spell check. Phone calls discouraged with query.

Q VOICE

PO Box 92385, Milwaukee, WI 53202
or
1661 N. Water Street Suite 411, Milwaukee, WI 53202
Regularity of Publication: Monthly
Phone Number: 414.278.7524   Fax Number: 414.272.7438
E-mail address: qvoice@aol.com
Publishers: William Attewell, Jorge L. Cabal
Editor in Chief: William Attewell

Quest - Wisconsin LesBiGayTrans Entertainment Guide

PO Box 1961, Green Bay, WI 54305
Regularity of Publication: Bi Weekly
Circulation: 7000   Audited: No
Phone Number(s):   800-578-3785 920-433-0611
Fax Number: Fax   920-433-0789
E-mail address: quest@quest-online.com
website address: quest-online.com
Publisher: Mark Mariucci
Advertising Manager: Theadore F. Witheril
Average length of feature: 800 words
Minimum rate paid per word: 3 cents
Minimum rate paid for photos: None allowed
How do you prefer your stories to be filed? Mac format or E-mail as
text message
How do you prefer to be contacted? E-mail or via phone
Special needs of your publication: Music reviews that are of interest to gay
men mostly and also lesbians.
What is the best advice for someone contemplating writing for your publication?
Most readers are bored with generic syndicated columns. Reading
should be entertaining even when it is to inform or educate.

Wisconsin Light

225 S. Second Street, Milwaukee, WI 53204
Regularity of Publication: Weekly
Circulation: 10,000
Audited: No – but pick up rate information is on file
Phone Number: (414) 226-0075
Fax Number: (414) 226-0096
E-mail address: wilight@aol.com   website address:www.wilight.com
Publisher: Greg Quindel
Editor: Bill Meunier editor@wilight.com
Arts Editor: Jerry Johnson
Advertising Manager: Greg Quindel
Average length of feature: words 800 -1200
Minimum rate paid per word: $15.00 per article
Minimum rate paid for photos: $10.00
How do you prefer your stories to be filed? Via email at editor@wilight.com
How do you prefer to be contacted? Email Bill Meunier at editor@wilight.com
Special needs of your publication: LGBT fashion and trends i.e.: clothes,
chic and trendy furniture etc., LGBT Health news, Political Cartoons,
celebrity interviews, LGBT Youth column and news, Lesbian news

International

ARGENTINA

Mundo Gay Magazine

M@G@Zine - Semanario de Mundo Gay
Complete mailing address: www.mundogay.com/magazine
Regularity of Publication: Weekly
E-mail address: magazine@mundogay.com
website address: www.mundogay.com/magazine
How do you prefer to be contacted?: by e-mail
Special needs of your publication: Gay and Lesbian Hispanic World News,
Essays, Humor, Important gay and lesbian news from the rest of the
world, Gay and Lesbian publications in Spanish,

AUSTRALIA

Adelaide Gay Times

Mortimer House
18 Freemasons Lane, Adelaide 5000   or
PO Box 10141 Gouger Street Adelaide 5000
Telephone: +61 08 8232 1544
Facsimile: +61 08 8232 1560
Email gt@adelaidegt.com.au   Website: www.adelaidegt.com.au

Bi The Way Adelaide

74 Coglin Street, Brompton 5007
Tel: (08) 8340 3538   E-mail: merlin@box.net.au

http://www.chariot.net.au/~merlin2/newsletter.html
Editor: Jason Squire

BlackOUT

(a newsletter by and for Aboriginal gay people)

PO Box 7, Darlinghurst, NSW 2010
Fax: (02) 9331 1199   E-mail to blackout@rocketmail.com
We publish everything in our newsletter (from poetry to what's on).

BrotherSister Newspaper

(Queensland)

210 Constance Street, Fortitude Valley, Queensland 4006
Regularity of Publication: Biweekly
Circulation:12,300   Audited: No
Phone Number: (07) 3852 2155
Fax Number: (07) 3852 2822
E-mail address: brosisq@thehub.com.au
website address: www.brothersister.com.au
Publisher: Bill Calder (03) 9429 8844 (ext. 15)
Managing Editor: Rebecca Freemantle
News Editor: Cristen Tilley
Advertising Manager: Brett Stevens and Peter Johnston
Average length of feature: 600 - 1000 words
Minimum rate paid per word: Standard $30 - $50 per feature story.
Minimum rate paid for photos: $15
How do you prefer your stories to be filed? mac formatted disc
How do you prefer to be contacted? email, phone or fax
Special needs of your publication: Feature articles that cover glbt issues.
Book reviews, theatre and movies. Health and Lifestyle issues,
celebrity interviews, album reviews. Legal Issues, parenting issues,
safe sex issues, work related issues.
What is the best advice for someone contemplating writing for your publication?
Make sure that the topic is relevant, confronting, and that it is
an issue that can be related to by as much of the general glbt
community as possible. Make sure that it is easily read - particularly
if it is a legal paper - that the jargon used kept to a minimum.

Brother Sister

(Victoria)

Suite 33A, 1st Floor, 261 Bridge Road, Richmond VIC 3121
Regularity of Publication: fortnightly (that's once every two weeks)
Circulation: 18,874   Audited: yes
Phone Number: 61 3 9429 8844   Fax Number: 61 3 9429 8966
E-mail address: brosisv@webtime.com.au
website address: http://www.brothersister.com.au
Publisher: Bill Calder ext 15
Managing Editor   Zoe Velonis ext 31
News Editor: James McKenzie ext 16
Advertising Manager   Toula Elefsiniotis ext 11,
                         Mark Whearem ext 12,
                         Shane Bridges ext 13
Average length of feature: about 1500 words
Minimum rate paid per word: Not applicable; we don't pay per word.
Payment negotiable on an individual basis.
How do you prefer your stories to be filed? Again, I prefer to negotiate this
with my contributors individually.
How do you prefer to be contacted? E-mail
What is the best advice for someone contemplating writing for your publication? We
don't really need contributors from outside Australia. The best way is
to read the paper and keep an eye out for ads saying contributors/
writers/photographers are needed and then to contact the Managing
Editor, preferably by snail mail with samples of work; if by email with
samples of work, do not send as attachments.

Capital Q Weekly

P.O. Box 981, Darlinghurst NSW 1300
Telephone: 61-2-9332-4988   Fax: 61-2-9380-5104
E-mail: capq@capitalq.com.au   Website: www.capitalq.com.au
Editor: Paul Hayes

InQUEERIES

critical inQueeries
P.O.Box 4472, Parkville 3052, Melbourne

Editors: Steven Angelides and Craig Bird
v-mail: 61(0)3 95372807 or 613 (0)412102359
fax: 61(0)3 93447894
e-mail: c.bird@pgrad.unimelb.edu.au or
                s.angelides@arts.unimelb.edu.au
The first fully-refereed academic journal of queer theory in Australia.
We are an interdisciplinary journal offering queer readings in the following areas: Cultural Studies, Feminist Theory, Film and Television,
Postcolonialism, Poststructuralism, Sexuality

Lesbians On The Loose

PO Box 1099, Darlinghurst, NSW 1300
Regularity of Publication : Monthly
Circulation: 20,000   Audited: No
Phone Number: +61 2 93806528
Fax Number: +61 2 93806529
E-mail address: lotl@lotl.com   website address: www.lotl.com
Average length of feature: 1,500 words
How do you prefer your stories to be filed? email
How do you prefer to be contacted? email
Special needs of your publication: National news/ local news/ Lesbian news
and views
What is the best advice for someone contemplating writing for your publication? Send
email outlining aims, ideas and experience ideally with example of
work attached.

National Biways Magazine

PO Box 490, Lutwyche, Brisbane, Queensland, 4030
Regularity of Publication: Bi-Monthly
Circulation: 300-400 (National) 100 (International)   Audited: No
Phone Number: +61-7-3857 2500
E-mail address: ausbinet@rainbow.net.au
website address: http://www.rainbow.net.au/~ausbinet/
Publisher: Australian Bisexual Network
Editor: Wayne Roberts
Average length of feature: 2-3 A4 pages 11 point, single spaced.
Minimum rate paid per word: voluntary contributions
Minimum rate paid for photos: voluntary contributions

How do you prefer your stories to be filed? e-mail
How do you prefer to be contacted? e-mail
Special needs of your publication: Bisexual stories, articles, news, Bi/Queer
Cartoons, Bi/Queer Book Reviews & Resources, GLBT International,
National and Local news, Bi Celebrity profiles, Bi Youth issues,
Partners of Bi People issues, Bi & GLBT Conferences & events
What is the best advice for someone contemplating writing for your publication?
Relevant news, stories, etc to the Bisexual Community
Our primary focus is for bisexual people and partners in Australia
followed by the Asia/Pacific region, then rest of the World. We are
also a keen advocate of GLBT rights issues and campaigns includ-
ing e-mail "Action Alerts"

Polare

The Editor, PO Box 266, Petersham, NSW 2029
Regularity of Publication: Bi-Monthly
Circulation: over 2000   Audited: No
Phone Number: (02) 9569 2366   Fax Number: (02) 9569 1176
E-mail address: gender@rainbow.net.au
Editor: George Andrews - (02) 9569 2366
Average length of feature: 1000 - 2000 words
How do you prefer to be contacted? Email or write
Special needs of your publication: Transgender/Transsexual issues;
gender-diversity
What is the best advice for someone contemplating writing for your publication?
Read some back issues of Polare to get the idea of what the
magazine is all about.

Sydney Star Observer

PO Box 939, Darlinghurst, NSW 1300
Regularity of Publication: Weekly
Circulation: 27,284   Audited:Yes (CAB audit)
Phone Number: (-61-2) 9380 5577   Fax Number: (-61-2) 9331 2118
E-mail address: mail@ssonet.com.au
website address: sso.rainbow.net.au
Publisher: Sydney Gay & Lesbian Community Publishing Ltd.
Editor: Vanessa McQuarrie (acting)
General Manager: Peter Dragicevich

Minimum rate paid per word: varies
Minimum rate paid for photos: varies

WestSide Observer

PO Box 131, North Perth, Western Australia 6006.
Tel. (08) 9242 2146   Fax (08) 9242 2209.
E-mail: editor@wso.com.au

Women Out West

PO Box 1121, West Leederville Western Australia 6901
Regularity of Publication: Monthly
Circulation: 3000   Audited: No
Phone Number:+ 61 8 9388 7673   Fax Number: + 61 8 9388 7673
E-mail address: outwest@iinet.net.au
Publisher: Outspoken Publications
Editor: Ruth Wykes
Features Editor: Lesley Sinagra
Advertising Manager: SueAnne Welch
Average length of feature: 2000 words
How do you prefer your stories to be filed? email or typed hard copy
How do you prefer to be contacted? any way - email is often easiest
Special needs of your publication: We are a lesbian magazine and will con-
sider publishing anything contemporary. We have a mix of issues,
lifestyle, performing and visual arts, cartoons, world, national and
local news, and profiles.
What is the best advice for someone contemplating writing for your publication?
Contact us to discuss idea, or submit work for consideration of being
published.

AUSTRIA

CONNECT

e-mail: connect@via.at   Website: www.via.at

168

LAMBDA-Nachrichten

Novaragasse 40, A-1020 Vienna,
Regularity of Publication: quarterly
Circulation: 1.000   Audited: No
Phone Number: +43-1-216 66 04; +43-1-545 13 10
Fax Number: + 43-1-216 66 04
E-mail address: office@hosiwien.at
website address: http://www.hosiwien.at
Publisher: Homosexuelle Initiative (HOSI) Wien
Editor: Kurt Krickler
Average length of feature: 1500-3000 words
Minimum rate paid per word: we don't/can't pay for stories
Minimum rate paid for photos: 50 US dollars
How do you prefer your stories to be filed? politics; "feuilleton";
How do you prefer to be contacted? By email.
Special needs of your publication: cartoons, humor, celebrity profiles, lesbian news and views, international news; NO novels, literary stories/features.

PRIDE

Das Gratismagazin der HOSI-Linz
Postfach 43, A-4013 Linz
Regularity of Publication: Bi-Monthly
Circulation: 3,000   Audited: No
Phone Number: 0043 732-60 98 981
Fax Number: 0043 732-60 98 981
E-mail address: hosi-linz@netway.at
website address: http://www.hosi-linz.gay.at
Publisher: HOSI-Linz
Editor: HOSI-Linz
Managing Editor: Gerhard Niederleuthner
Features Editor: Gernot Wartner
Arts Editor: Gerhard Niederleuthner
News Editor: Gernot Wartner
Advertising Manager: Gernot Wartner

Average length of feature: 1800 words
Minimum rate paid per word: without any payment

Minimum rate paid for photos: without any payment
How do you prefer your stories to be filed? Windows or Mac compatible
How do you prefer to be contacted? Phone, Fax or e-mail
Special needs of your publication: Cartoons, celebrity profiles, lesbian news and views

XTRA!

PostFach 77, 1043 Wien
Phone: 0664/278 31 61   E-mail: xtra@magnet.at
Website: www.xtra.gay.at

BELGIUM

Gay Mag

Graphics & Media
Rue des Teinturiers, 18 b7 B-1000 Brussels
gm@skynet.be

BRAZIL

HOMO SAPIENS - Grupo Gay da Bahia, Brazil

C.POSTAL 2552, 40022-260, SALVADOR, BAHIA,
Regularity of Publication: Bi-Monthly
Circulation: 1.000
Phone Number :55-71-322.2262   Fax Number: 55-71-322.3782
E-mail address: luizmott@ufba.br   website address: www.ggb.org.br
Publisher: 55-71-3223782
Editor: 55-71-3222262
Arts Editor: 55-71-9894748
News Editor: 55-71-994-0757
Minimum rate paid per word:5 cents
Minimum rate paid for photos:1

How do you prefer to be contacted? by email
Special needs of your publication: coverage of racial minority issues

CANADA

Capital Extra

177 Nepean Street, Suite 506, Ottawa ON K2P 0B4
Regularity of Publication: monthly
Circulation: 20,000
Phone Number: (613) 237 7133   Fax Number: (613) 237 6651
E-mail address: CAPXTRA@XTRA.CA
Publisher and Editor: Brandon Matheson
Advertising Manager: George Hartsgrove

DRAGUN magazine

P.O. Box #607 50 Charles St. East, Toronto, Ontario, M4Y 2L8
Regularity of Publication: Quarterly: Feb/May/August/November
Premiere issue circulation (June 1999) is 10, 000 Projected circula-
tion by June 2000, 40,000   Audited: No but soon to be
Phone Number: (416) 737. 5538
E-mail address: jtran@dragunmagazine.com
website address: www.dragunmagazine.com
Publisher: Jimm Tran (416) 737. 5538
Senior Editor: Joshua Kreig
Associate Editor: Duc Nguyen
Creative Director: Michael Chambers
Art Director: Nick Vongthavy
Advertising Manager: Jimm Tran/ Tim Ylmaz
Average length of feature: inclusive of media and photos 4-6 pages.
Minimum rate paid per word: variable/ to be negotiated
Minimum rate paid for photos: variable/ to be negotiated
How do you prefer your stories to be filed? Microsoft WORD files,
How do you prefer to be contacted? Email : jtran@dragunmagazine.com
Special needs of your publication: cartoons, humor, book reviews, national
gay Asian relevant news issues. We are about 65% Gay Asian in
content, 35% is anything else, other cultures. DRAGUN magazine is

a Lifestyle magazine catering to the Gay and Lesbian Asian Community and their friends. Some regular features are: feature articles, fashion spreads, health, technology, Japanese Animation, entertainment/music, Celebrity profiles, paparazzi spreads etc. *What is the best advice for someone contemplating writing for your publication?* Send us some examples of your writing/photography/illustrations via email. Keep size and format of images to a minimum (JPEG, GIF files are acceptable).

Exclaim!

7-B Pleasant Blvd., Unit #966, Toronto, Ontario M4T 1K2
Regularity of Publication: Monthly   Circulation: 106,780
Phone Number: (416) 535 9735   Fax Number: (416) 535 0566
E-mail address: exclaim@exclaim.ca
website address: http://www.exclaim.ca
Publisher: Ian Danzig
Managing Editor: James Keast   james@exclaim.ca
West Coast Editor: Denise Sheppard   exclaim.west@exclaim.ca
Advertising: John Schweigel, Tommy Goodwin,
          Jon Bartlett exclaim@exclaim.ca

fab

25 Wood Street, Suite #104, Toronto, ON M4Y 2PQ
Regularity of Publication Biweekly
Circulation: 20,000   Audited: No
Phone Number: 416 599 9273   Fax Number: 416 599 0964
E-mail address: fabto@hotmail.com
Publisher: Michael Schwarz
Editor: John Kennedy
Advertising Manager: Allan S. Kay
Average length of feature: 1000 words
Minimum rate paid per word: 10 cents (CDN)
Minimum rate paid for photos: $10 CDN
How do you prefer your stories to be filed? e-mail or diskette
How do you prefer to be contacted? e-mail
Special needs of your publication: Arts and entertainment, gay issues, health, recreation, etc
What is the best advice for someone contemplating writing for your publication? send

outline by email to the editor. We do not accept poetry or fiction.

FAB National

110 Spadina Avenue, Suite 301, Toronto ON M5V 2K4
Regularity of Publication: Bi-monthly
Circulation: 40,000   Audited: No
Phone Number: (416) 306-0180   Fax Number: (416) 306-0182
E-mail address: fab@myna.com
website address: www.fabmag.com
Publisher: Keir MacRae
Editor: Jim Armstrong
Advertising Manager: Marc Rutherford
Market/Style Editor: Sue Forster
Art Director: Matt Ross
Average length of feature: 1500 words
Minimum rate paid per word: negotiable
Minimum rate paid for photos: negotiable
How do you prefer your stories to be filed? e-mail
How do you prefer to be contacted? e-mail or snail-mail
Special needs of your publication: We are not looking for reviews or time-sensitive articles.
What is the best advice for someone contemplating writing for your publication?
Read a copy. Submission guidelines are available upon request.

FUGUES

Published in French, Fugues is Quebec's leading publication (with some local articles in English) of the gay and lesbian community. Founded in 1984 and based in Montreal, it is a digest size monthly.
1212, rue Saint-Hubert, Montreal, Quebec, H2L 3Y7
Regularity of Publication Monthly
Circulation 50 000 copies   Audited: No (Sworn statement by publisher)
Phone Number (514) 848-1854   Fax Number (514) 845-7645
E-mail addresses   info@fugues.com
                     redaction@fugues.com
                     publicite@fugues.com
website address   http://www.fugues.com
Please give both the name and the telephone extension or direct

line: There is only one phone number, (514) 848-1854
Publisher   Martin Hamel
Editor in chief   Yves Lafontaine
Advertising Manager   Real Lefebvre
Average length of feature: 500 to 2,000 words
We have three staff writers (on salary) and several freelancers on a fixed remuneration
How do you prefer to be contacted? Before the writing of an article. We like to discuss the angle...
Special needs of your publication: None that aren't fulfilled for the moment.
What is the best advice for someone contemplating writing for your publication?
To contact us with an idea. We will see if this is something of interest for us and our readers

The Guard Mag

100 - 323 Somerset Street West, Ottawa, Ontario, K2P 0J8
Regularity of Publication: Monthly
Circulation: 20,000 copies in Ottawa, Montreal, and Toronto
Audited: No
Phone Number: 613-565-0347   Fax Number: 613-565-4045
E-mail address: info@theguardmag.com
website address: www.theguardmag.com
Publisher: Boumer Publications
Editor: Robert Mercier
Advertising Manager: Michel Boucher
Average length of feature: words 750
Minimum rate paid per word: Negotiable
Minimum rate paid for photos: $9
How do you prefer your stories to be filed? email or diskette(word)
How do you prefer to be contacted? telephone or email
Special needs of your publication: Local and national news of a non-politicial nature, celebrity profiles, current events, music/film/video/book reviews
What is the best advice for someone contemplating writing for your publication? Be as non-political as possible, be as upbeat as possible (nothing negative)

ICON Magazine

467 Church Street, Second Floor North, Toronto, Ontario M4Y 2C5

Regularity of Publication: Monthly
Phone Number: (416) 960 9607   1-888-444-ICON
Fax Number: (416) 960 0655
E-mail address: iconmag@inforamp.net
website address: www.iconmagazine.com
Publisher and Editor-In-Chief: Brad Walker
Associate Editor: Aaron Martin
Director of Advertising: Paul Vella

Lavender Rhinoceros

P.O. Box 5339, Station B, Victoria, BC V8R 6S4
Regularity of Publication: monthly
Circulation: 1,000 or more   Audited: No
Phone Number:(250)598-6490   Fax Number:as above, phone first
E-mail address: lavrhino@home.com
Publisher: Barbara McLauchlin (250) 598-6490
Editor: Barbara McLauchlin with Michael Yoder
Average length of feature: 500 to 800 words
Minimum rate paid per word: C$50 per article
Minimum rate paid for photos: C$12
How do you prefer your stories to be filed? e-mail
How do you prefer to be contacted? e-mail
Special needs of your publication: any issue if transformative or if it has a large impact that could affect us here on Vancouver Island or in Canada as a whole.
What is the best advice for someone contemplating writing for your publication? Keep to deadline--1st of month prior to publication, 500 words is best and keep to tight copy. Opinions count but interested in facts, news style.

LIMBO - Canada's National Lesbian Magazine

P.O. Box 21035, Paris, Ontario, N3L 3R0
Regularity of Publication: Bi-monthly
Circulation: 4000   Audited:Yes
Phone Number: 519-458-8297
Fax Number: 519-458-8448
E-mail address: publisher@limbo.ca;   editor@limbo.ca;
                       art@limbo.ca;   marketing@limbo.ca;

photo@limbo.ca;   kelly@limbo.ca
website address: www.limbo.ca
Publisher and Editor : Anne Gecas, 519-458-8297
Managing Editor: Kerry Turcotte, 519-458-8297
Advertising Manager: Dan Bowers, 416-962-9696
                     fax: 416-972-7497
                     email: danbowes@powerarts.com
Average length of feature: 2500 words
How do you prefer to be contacted? Submissions by post
Special needs of your publication: Lesbian news and views, general interest
stories, fashion related material, women's health issues
What is the best advice for someone contemplating writing for your publication? Have
fun with it.

OUTLOOKS

Box 439, Suite #100, 1039 17th Avenue SW, Calgary AB T2T 0B2
Monthly
Phone: 403 228 1157 toll free 1-888 228 1157
Fax: 403 228 7735
E-mail: outlooks@cadvision.com
Website   www.outlooks.ab.ca
Circulation 25,500
Advertising: Doug McDougall   dougalld@cadvision.com

QC Magazine

Box 64292, 5512-4th Street NW, Calgary AB T2K 6J1
Phone: 403 630 2061   Fax: 403 275 6443
E-mail: qcmag@home.com   website: www.nucleus.com/~qcmag
Publisher/Editor in Chief: Shelagh Anderson
Managing Editor: Monica Piros

RG (Magazine)

P.O. Box 915, Station C, Montreal H2L 4V2
Regularity of Publication: MONTHLY
Circulation: 55000   Audited: No
Phone Number:514 - 523 - 9463   Fax Number: 514 523-2214

E-mail address: rgmag@colba.net
website address: www.colba.net/rgmag/
Publisher and Editor: Alain Bouchard   514-523-9463
Average length of feature: 700 - 1000 words
How do you prefer to be contacted? E-MAIL

Times .10 Magazine

10121-124 Street, Edmonton, AB T5N 1P5
Phone: 780 415 5616   888 TIMES10
Fax: 780 455 6540
E-mail: dcambly@v-wave.com   Website: www.times10.org
10 issues annually
Managing Editor: Dennis Cambly
Features Editor: Lorelei Donahue
Arts Editor: Gib Adams
Advertising manager: Jacy Dobrich
Length of feature: 300 words
How do you prefer your stories to be filed? Word 97
E-mail address: times10@v-wave.com
We are a non-profit society and have limited funding.
Circulation: 7,000   Audited: No

Treize: revue lesbienne

C.P.771, Succ. C, Montreal, Qc, H2L 4L6
Regularity of Publication : 3 times a year
Circulation: 500 mainly in Quebec
E-mail address: treize@morag.com
website address: http://www.morag.com/treize/
Publisher: Les Editions Hystéria (non-profit organisation)
To contact Editor, Arts Director, Advertising Manager, Distribution
Manager please use postal or e-mail addresses given above.
Average length of feature: 6 000 char.
How do you prefer your stories to be filed? electronic document
How do you prefer to be contacted? e-mail
Special needs of your publication: Treize is a French lesbian publication
from Quebec welcoming any women/lesbian material aiming at a
lesbian readership. English material sent will be translated in French
if published. Visual material (pictures, illustrations) specially welcome.

What is the best advice for someone contemplating writing for your publication? Treize is dedicated to lesbian culture and life style of all ages. Since we are a non-profit organisation, all work is done on a volunteer basis, but Treize is faithfully read by a growing number of lesbians throughout Quebec and even abroad.

VICE Magazine

124 McGill Suite 400, Montreal, Quebec H2Y 2E5
Phone: 514 397 9518   Fax: 514 397 0083
E-mail: vicenet@total.net   Website: www.total.net/~vicenet
Published ten times a year
Circulation: 60,000
Publishers: Suroosh Alvi,   Gavin McInnes,   Shane Smith

The Voice Magazine

P.O. Box 24015, RPO, Evergreen, Kitchener, Ontario, N2M 5P1
Regularity of Publication: Monthly   Audited: No
Phone Number: 519-743-5015   Fax Number: same
E-mail address: thevoice@thevoice.on.ca
website address: http://www.thevoice.on.ca
Publisher and Editor: Ms. A.J. Mahari   519-743-5015
Advertising Manager: Lyn McGinnis   519-747-5848
Average length of feature: 500-700 words
Minimum rate paid per word: Don't pay per word
Minimum rate paid for photos: Negotiable
How do you prefer your stories to be filed? Email
How do you prefer to be contacted? Email or phone
Special needs of your publication: Gay/Lesbian issues, Humour, Cartoons, Reviews, Local News, Profiles, Issues that affect all of our lives.
What is the best advice for someone contemplating writing for your publication? Get in touch with us. Currently we are new and not paying much if at all for copy. Let us know what you write. We are in Canada and prefer issues that interest our local readers (Southern Ontario).If you are elsewhere we are not interested in news and views related to other local areas. General articles on issues are always welcome. At the time of filing this we have published seven issues and do not pay for submissions. We hope to be in a position to do so in a few months time.

WAYVES

PO Box 34090, Scotia Square, Halifax NS B3J 3S1
Phone: 902 827 3969   E-mail: wayves@fox.nstn.ca
Website: www.chebucto.ns.ca/CommunitySupport/Wayves
Published 10 times a year by a non-profit collective
Advertising: Kim Vance/Charlene Vacon

XTRA!

491 Church Street #200, Toronto ON M4Y 2C6
Phone: 416 925 6665   800 268 XTRA
Fax: 416 925 6674   E-mail: david.walberg@xtra.ca
Website: www.xtra.ca
Bi-weekly
Published by   Pink Triangle Press
Publisher & Editor in chief: David Walberg

XTRA! West

501-1033 Davie street, Vancouver BC, V6E 1M7
Regularity of Publication: BI WEEKLY
Circulation: 30,000   Audited: No
Phone Number: 604 684 9696   Fax Number: 604 684 9697
E-mail address: XWEDITOR@xtra.ca
website address: www.xtra.org
Publisher: (ext. 28)
Managing Editor: Gareth Kirkby (ext.24)
Arts Editor: (ext.3   )
Advertising Manager: Michael Clancey (ext. 23)
Average length of feature: 1400 words
Minimum rate paid per word: 12 cents (Canadian)
Minimum rate paid for photos: $50 (Canadian)
How do you prefer your stories to be filed? e-mail
How do you prefer to be contacted? e-mail
Special needs of your publication: Humor, Lesbian news and views
What is the best advice for someone contemplating writing for your publication?
We're a very sex-positive newspaper. We write a lot about public sex
importance of porn, etc, as well as local and national queer news

and views and sexual politics.

COSTA RICA

GENTE 10

PO Box 1910-2100, Guadalupe, Costa Rica
Regularity of Publication: Bimonthly.
Circulation: 3000
Phone Number: (506) 285-5368   Fax Number: (506) 285-5368
E-mail address: jorgon@sol.racsa.co.cr

Publisher: Jose Carrasquero Diaz
Editor: Jorge Gonzalez Calvo
Arts Editor: Jose Carrasquero
Advertising Manager: Jorge Gonzalez Calvo
How do you prefer your stories to be filed? email
How do you prefer to be contacted? E-mail: jorgon@sol.racsa.co.cr
Special needs of your publication: Cartoons, Humor, Celebrity profiles,
Health issues, Lesbian news and views, Travel issues. We need lots
of photos of everything!
WE NEED ADVERTIZERS.
What is the best advice for someone contemplating writing for your publication?
Better in Spanish but English will do ok.

THE CZECH REPUBLIC

AMIGO

P.O. Box 60, CZ- 180 21, Praha 8
e-mail: amigo@czn.cz

180

FINLAND

Z

Hietalahdenkatu 2 B 16, 00180 Helsinki, Finland
Regularity of Publication: BiMonthly
Phone Number(s):   +358-9-6123244,   +358-40-7544014
Fax Number: +358-9-6123266
E-mail address: editor@seta.fi
website address: http://www.seta.fi/z
Publisher: SETA Seksuaalinen tasavertaisuus ry.
Editor: Pauli Löija   +358-9-6123244,
+358-40-7544014
Advertising Manager: Marko Stenroos +358-9-6123245
Average length of feature:1000-15000 words
Minimum rate paid per word: - (usually nothing)
Minimum rate paid for photos: - (usually nothing)
How do you prefer your stories to be filed? by e-mail
How do you prefer to be contacted? by e-mail
Special needs of your publication: Book Reviews, Celebrity profiles, Gay and Lesbian news and views
What is the best advice for someone contemplating writing for your publication? One must write in Finnish!

FRANCE

Double Face

99 rue de la Verrerie, 75004 Paris France
Phone: 01 48 04 58 00   Fax:01 48 04 05 92
E-Mail: groupeillico@mail2.imaginet.fr
Publisher: Jacky Fougeray
Editor in Chief: Jean-Francois Laforgerie

Agenda Projet X

PX PRESSE
Immeuble Métropole 19 134-140, rue d'Aubervilliers F-75019, Paris France
Regularity of Publication :   Monthly
Circulation:4,500   Audited: No
Phone Number: 33/(0)1 53 35 98 50
Fax Number: 33/(0)1 53 35 98 80
E-mail address: projetx@projetx.com
website address: http://www.projetx.com/

Publisher: Joël Hladinynk 33/(0)1 53 35 98 50
Editor: Eric Lapôtre   33/(0)1 53 35 98 55
Advertising Manager: Jérôme Aznar 33/(0)1 53 35 98 71
How do you prefer to be contacted? email / Fax
Special needs of your publication: Everything connected with
hard/leather/fetish gay sex - cartoons, stories, pictures, models..
What is the best advice for someone contemplating writing for your publication?
Money shouldn't be the first motivation to contact us, but dedication to
pleasure should be ! A good open door to make a name in Europe.

THE AGENDA

Complete mailing address: as above
Regularity of Publication: Monthly
Circulation: 20,000   Audited: No
Phone Number :as above   Fax Number: as above
E-mail address:as above   website address:as above
Publisher/editor...   as above
How do you prefer to be contacted?   as above
Special needs of your publication: Informations on specific
leather/hard/sm/fetish topics (exhibitions, books, websites, interna-
tional news that could interest European readers, goods, media,
press etc.)

Question de Genre/GKC

BP 36 59009 Lille cedex
Regularity of Publication: quarterly

Circulation: 1000   Audited: No
Phone Number(s):   (33) 03 20 06 33 941
Fax Number(s):   (33) 03 20 78 18 76
E-mail address: GKC@worldnet.fr

Têtu

88 bis, rue du faubourg du Temple, 75011, Paris, France
Regularity of Publication :   Monthly
Circulation: 50.000 copies   Audited: Yes
Phone Number: 01 43 14 71 60   Fax Number: 01 43 14 64 64
E-mail address: tetu@tetu.com
website address: http://www.tetu.com
Publishers :   Pierre Bergé / Christophe Girard
Editor :   Thomas Doustaly (ext. 68)
Art Director :   La Shampouineuse (aka Michel Poulain)
Assistant editor (Music, Arts, Motion pictures, TV) : Patrick Thévenin
News Editor :   Judith Silberfeld
Advertising Manager : Norbert Pochon (ext. 67)
Minimum rate paid per word: We don't pay per word in France. We pay 200 FF for 1.500 signs (a sign is a letter, a space between two words, or a punctuation)
Minimum rate paid for photos: 1000 FF for a full page, 500 FF for half a page
How do you prefer to be contacted ? By mail
What is the best advice for someone contemplating writing for your publication ? To be honest, professional and to watch permanently the most exciting topics in politics, fashion, arts and social life to write about.

GERMANY

HINNERK

Koppel 97, 20099 Hamburg
Tel. (040) 24 06 45   Fax: (040) 24 06 50
e-mail: redaktion@hinnerk.de
Website: www.hinnerk.de
Editors: Burkhard Knopke, Jens von Häfen

QUEER - Germany's leading Gay & Lesbian newspaper

Postbox 29 02 44, D-50524 Köln, Germany 33
Regularity of Publication: monthly
Circulation: 85,000 copies   Audited: Yes (by IVW)
Phone Number: +49 221 579 76-0
Fax Number: +49 221 579 76-66
E-mail address: queer@pride.de
website address: www.queer.de (under construction)
Publisher: Micha Schulze, -76
Editor: Christian Scheuß, 10
Managing Editor: Christian Scheuß, -10
Features Editor: Marc Kersten, -20
Arts Editor: Christian Scheuß, -10
News Editor: Marc Kersten, -20
Advertising Manager: Helmut Ladwig, -40
Average length of feature: 10000 letters
Minimum rate paid per word: 0,65 DM per line
Minimum rate paid for photos: 45 DM
How do you prefer your stories to be filed? doc
How do you prefer to be contacted? eMail
Special needs of your publication: International news and features, interviews with prominent persons
What is the best advice for someone contemplating writing for your publication? just send an eMail...

lespress

kaiser-karl-ring 57, d-53111 Bonn, Germany
Regularity of Publication: monthly
Circulation: 10,000   Audited: No
Phone Number(s):   +49 228 653464, +49 228 653475
Fax Number: +49 228 653501
E-mail address: info@lespress.de
website address: http://www.lespress.de
Publisher: Anhamm + Richrath (+49 228 653464)
Editor: Anhamm + Richrath (info@lespress.de)
Managing Editor: U. Anhamm   (u.anhamm@lespress.de)
Features Editor: M. Richrath   (m.richrath@lespress.de)

Arts Editor: S. Sellier   (litera@lespress.de)
News Editor: U. Anhamm   (lesmopol@lespress.de)
Advertising Manager: C. Gekeler   (kaz@lespress.de)
Average length of feature: 5,000 words
Minimum rate paid per letter: 0.01 DM per word
Minimum rate paid for photos: 20 DM
How do you prefer your stories to be filed? RTF
How do you prefer to be contacted? per e-mail
Special needs of your publication: Cartoons, International Celebrity profiles, Lesbian news and views.
What is the best advice for someone contemplating writing for your publication? Send us a feature/story via e-mail (info@lespress.de) plus a brief introduction.

Sergej

Kopehhagener Strasse 14, Berlin 10437
Regularity of Publication: Monthly
Circulation: 103,000
Phone Number: ++ 49 -30 - 443 198-0 Fax Number: -77 / -22
E-mail address: sergej@pride.de   website address: www.sergej.de
Publisher: Sergej Medien Verlag
Editor: Carsten Heider
Managing Editor: Markus Hagel (ext. 11)
Advertising Manager: Sebastian Pleißner (ext. 33)
How do you prefer to be contacted? e-mail
Special needs of your publication: Cartoons - National news - local news
What is the best advice for someone contemplating writing for your publication? Short texts, lots of information, only in German language.

GREECE

DEON

website: www.deon.gr

OPOTHOS

POB 10839 GR-541 10 Thessaloniki GREECE
Telephone: +(095) 366 281   Fax: +(031) 763 906
Wednesdays 21:00-23:00 local time
e-mail: opoth@ilga.org
For more information, submissions, contributions, personal ads, etc,
write to the OPOTH, P.O. Box:10839, G.R.:54110, Thessaloniki,
(please, omit the name OPOTH if sending big packages), We
publish the "O Pothos" ("Disire") magazine about once a year.
The aim of the magazine is to be a forum of authentic thought and
questioning regarding homosexuality - mainly about its sustained
oppression as an amorous choice.

Romeo

88, Ippokratous Street, G.R.11472, Athens Greece.
tel.: 364 29 11, 364 29 12, 364 29 13.

TO KRAXIMO

P.O. Box 4228 10210 Athens
Phone: 365 22 49

HUNGARY

Labrisz

H-1554 Budapest,
Regularity of Publication: quarterly
Phone Number: +36 1 350 9650   Fax Number: + 36 1 350 9650
E-mail address: hatter@interware.hu
Contact person: Bea Sandor, above addresses
Average length of feature: 200 to 500 words
We won't be able to pay, our funding is only enough for printing, and

there is not a huge audience to buy and support the magazine... the 50-60 out lesbians in Hungary are not a mass
How do you prefer your stories to be filed? e-mail or fax
How do you prefer to be contacted? e-mail or fax

MASOK

P.O. Box 388 1461 Budapest
Phone & Fax: 266 99 59   Monthly

Szuper Erosz

P.O. Box 1242 1242 Budapest
Monthly

INDIA

BOMBAY DOST

105 Veena Beena Shopping Centre Bandra Station Road, Bandra (West), Mumbai 400,050, INDIA
Regularity of Publication: Quarterly
Phone Number: 640 4741/ 618 7476   Fax Number: 651 4955
E-mail address: pppltd@yahoo.com
website address: www.humsafar.org
Publisher and Editor: Ashok Row Kavi   (91.22) 646 3590
Average length of feature: 1500 words
Minimum rate paid per word: Depending on the feature (Rs. 500 being the average)
Minimum rate paid for photos: (Rs. 50 per photograph)
How do you prefer your stories to be filed? By e-mail, double spaced and word-count specificed.
How do you prefer to be contacted? By e-mail at pppltd@yahoo.com
Special needs of your publication: Everything and anything about gay/ lesbian/bisexual/transgender life relevant to India and Asia
What is the best advice for someone contemplating writing for your publication? Please understand the problems of the invisible community in India

and look at the emerging gay identity.

Darpan "The Newsletter of the Humrahi Group"

E-mail: aka9@hotmail.com
Website: www.geocities.com/WestHollywood/Heights/7258/

INDONESIA

GAYa NUSANTARA

Jalan Mulyosari Timur 46, Surabaya 60112, INDONESIA
Regularity of Publication: bimonthly
Circulation: 700   Audited: No
Phone Number: +62 31 593 4924; +62 811 311743 (mobile)
Fax Number: +62 31 599 3569
E-mail address: gayanusa@ilga.org
website address: welcome.to/gaya
Publisher: Dede Oetomo
Editor: Ibhoed
Managing Editor: Ruddy Mustapha, Awan
Features Editor: Ibhoed
Arts Editor: Oetomo, Ibhoed
News Editor: Dede Oetomo
Advertising Manager: Dede Oetomo
Average length of feature: 2,000 words
Minimum rate paid per word: two free copies of magazine containing contribution
Minimum rate paid for photos: two free copies of magazine containing contribution
How do you prefer your stories to be filed? by email
How do you prefer to be contacted? by email
Special needs of your publication: Indonesia-related items. Items in English or languages other than Indonesian will be translated into Indonesian.
What is the best advice for someone contemplating writing for your publication?
Just try writing.

188

IRELAND

Gay Community News (GCN)

6 South William Street, Dublin 2
Tel +353 1 671 093   fax 671 354
Email: gcn@tinet.ie

Hot Press

13 Trinity Street, Dublin 2
Tel + 353 1 679 5077   Fax: + 353 1 679 5097

Women's News - Irelands Feminist Monthly

30 Donegall Street, Belfast BT1 2GQ, Northern Ireland
Regularity of Publication: monthly
Circulation: 4000   Audited: No
Phone Number: (01232) 322823   Fax Number: (01232) 438788
E-mail address: womensnews@dnet.co.uk
website address: www.d-n-a.net/users/dnetWeZM
Advertising Manager: Adele Grey, Michelle Hayes
Women's News acts as collective and and its up to the collective to
make editorial decisions.
Average length of feature: 550 words
Minimum rate paid per word: we are not in the position to pay for
contributions
How do you prefer your stories to be filed? email as txt.doc., or floppy saved
as txt.
How do you prefer to be contacted? email, phone, fax
Special needs of your publication: Lesbian news and views, coverage of
racial minority issues, book reviews, cartoons, humor
What is the best advice for someone contemplating writing for your publication? We
are the only feminist monthly in Ireland and cover lesbian issues. We
have a readership in Ireland, UK, Europe and a few overseas. Our
deadline is the 10th of the month before publishing, for ads its the
5th. Our advertising rates are very attractive. We welcome contribu-

tions and would encourage women to send us their articles/pieces by email or by snail-mail (if not time restricted).

ITALY

BABILONIA

Via Astura 8, 20141 Milano
Tel. 02-5696468   Fax 02-55213419
e-mail: babilonia@iol.it
website: www.babilonia.net

JAPAN

Outragous Tokyo (Tokyo, Japan)

http://shrine.cyber.ad.jp/~darrell/outr/home/outr-home.html
Japan's first free English-language gay magazine. We are not a translation of Japanese magazines. Outrageous Tokyo is unique in that it is a forum to exchange ideas and opinions, learn more about what's going on in Tokyo, and work toward creating a more vibrant and cohesive gay community in Japan

KOREA

BUDDY

e-mail: buddy79@buddy79.com   Website: www.buddy79.com
Monthly

Chingusai

"Among Friends" is Korea's first gay magazine. It is available at the

gay bars. Korean language.
Joong-ku Shindang 5 dong 142-5,
Sung-hwan Building A-411
Seoul 100-455, Korea
Tel.Fax.   82-2-232-2379
Editor-in-Chief: Sang-hei Park,

MEXICO

Boys & Toys

Azul Editions
Apdo postal 716, CP 06002, Mexico City

Sergay

E-mail: sergay@sergay.com.mx   Website: www.sergay.com.mx

NETHERLANDS

De Gay Krant

Best Publishing Group
P.O. Box 10, 5680 AA BEST The Netherlands
Circulation: 30,500
Phone: + 31 499 39 10 00   Fax: + 31 499 37 26 38
Editorial fax: + 31 499 39 06 03
E-mail Editors: redactie@gaykrant.nl

Expreszo

P.O. Box 3836, 1001 AP, Amsterdam The Netherlands
Regularity of Publication: Bi-monthly

Circulation: 7,000 copies   Audited: No
Phone Number: +31 20 6234596   Fax Number: +31 20 6267795
E-mail address: info@expreszo.nl
website address: www.expreszo.nl
Publisher: Stichting Hoezo
Editor: Caspar Pisters
Advertising Manager: Sander Groen
Average length of feature: 1200 words
Minimum rate paid per word: varies
Minimum rate paid for photos: varies
How do you prefer your stories to be filed? WP 5.1 (DOS)
How do you prefer to be contacted? by e-mail, snail mail or fax

Gay News Amsterdam

1e Helmersstraat 17, P.O. Box 76609, 1070 HE Amsterdam,
The Netherlands
Publisher: Gay International Press,
Fax: +31 20 675 38 61   Email: info@gaynews.nl
Amsterdam's largest gay publication, bi-lingual.

MADAM

Rozenstraat, 14 1016 NX Amsterdam
E-mail: madamekk@dds.nl   http://www.dds.nl/~madamekk/

SQUEEZE

Postbus 8671, 3009 Rotterdam, Netherlands
Regularity of Publication   Monthly
Circulation: 30,000
Phone Number: 010 4525082   Fax Number: 010 4525 768
E-mail address: redactie@squeeze.nl
website address: www.squeeze.nl
Publisher: Maximum Media
Editor: Edwin Reinerie
Fashion Editor: Alex van der Steen
Advertising Manager: Media Movements, Amsterdam
Average length of feature: 2000 words

How do you prefer to be contacted? **e-mail**
Special needs of your publication: International lifestyle. No social issues
What is the best advice for someone contemplating writing for your publication?
Send as many ideas on gay lifestyle issues as possible.

XL Monthly Magazine of COC

Postbus 3836, 1001 AP Amsterdam
or
Rozenstraat 8, Amsterdam
tel.   020 623 45 96   fax: 020 626 77 95.
Editor: Marleen Slob   Email: mhslob@xs4all.nl

Zij aan Zij (for lesbians and bisexual women)

Postbus 3218, 2280 GE Rijswijk
Phone: 070 3988800   Fax: 070 3988635
E-mail: redactie@zijaanzij.nl   website: www.zijaanzij.nl/
Editor: Ria van Oosten (hoofdredacteur)

NEW ZEALAND

express newspaper

PO Box 47-514, Ponsonby, Auckland, New Zealand
Regularity of Publication: Biweekly
Circulation: 6,787   Audited: Yes
Phone Number: 64-9-361 0190   Fax Number: 64-9-361 0191
E-mail address: express@outnet.co.nz
website address: gaynz.com/express
Chief executive,   Cornerstone Publications: Mark Graham
Editor: Claire Gummer
Advertising Manager: Joanne Carnachan
Average length of feature: 900 words
Minimum rate paid per word: to be negotiated
Minimum rate paid for photos: to be negotiated
How do you prefer your stories to be filed? by e-mail, as message text rather

than attachments
How do you prefer to be contacted? by e-mail from overseas, otherwise
by phone
Special needs of your publication: Largely New Zealand gay and lesbian
news, with strong local arts coverage.
What is the best advice for someone contemplating writing for your publication?
Contact us first!

OUT! Magazine

Private Bag 92126, Auckland 1. New Zealand
Regularity of Publication: BI MONTHLY
Circulation: 8000
Phone Number: (64) (9) 377 9031   Fax Number:(64) (9) 377 7767
E-mail address: out@nz.com   website address: nz.com/glb/OUT/
Publisher: TONY KATAVICH   (64) (9) 377 9031
Editor: BRETT SHEPPARD   (64) (9) 377 9031
Average length of feature: 1000 words
Minimum rate paid per word: BY ARRANGEMENT
Minimum rate paid for photos: BY ARRANGEMENT
How do you prefer your stories to be filed? EMAIL
How do you prefer to be contacted?   EMAIL
What is the best advice for someone contemplating writing for your publication?
CONTACT FOR NEEDS

NORWAY

BLIKK

Postboks 6838, St Olavs Plass, 0130 Oslo
Phone: 011 47 2220 2220   Fax: 011 47 2236 2803
Monthly

POLAND

GEJZER Magazine/Nowy Men Magazine

(same adresses, phones and people)
Nowy Men, Pink Press
Box 15800-975 Warszawa 12 Poland
Regularity of Publication: Monthly
Circulation: 20.000   Audited: No
Phone Number: + 48 22 868-54-16, + 48 22 868-54-02,
                                   + 48 22 868-54-08
Fax Number: + 48 22 868-54-17 (ask for fax)
E-mail address: starosta@supermedia.pl
Publisher: all above   (ext. 104)
Editor: (ext. 220)
News Editor: (ext. 219)
Advertising Manager: (ext. 221)

PORTUGAL

KORPUS

Rua da Ilha Terceira, 34 - R/c 1000 Lisbon Portugal
Publisher and Editor: Isidoro Sousa
Mobile: +351-936-5086300   Telephone: +351-1-3151323

RUSSIA

ARGO

P.O.Box 12, c/o V.GOUS'KOV 111402, Moscow,
Regularity of Publication: 1-2 per year
Circulation: 5000   Audited: NO

Phone Number: (7-095) 370-6752   Fax Number: (7-095) 370-6752
E-mail address: argorisk@glasnet.ru
Minimum rate paid per word: private ads of 20 words - free
How do you prefer your stories to be filed? E-mail
How do you prefer to be contacted? E-mail

1/10

Att: Alexander Prokofiev,
111123, Moscow E-123
Good quality publication. 36 pages. Published bimonthly. USD 6
p/copy.
Tel: (095) 305-5737

RISK

PO BOX 12, 111402 Moscow
Literary almanac. 116 pages. Published 2 times a year. USD 8 p/copy.
Tel/fax (095) 370-6752.   e-mail:argorisk@glas.apc.org

TREUGOLNIK

PO Box 7, 105037 Moscow.
Information bulletin edited by Treugolnik (Triangle) society covering all
gay related issues, especially political ones, struggle for gay rights.
Tel: (095) 153-8002   e-mail: triangle@glas.apc.org

URANUS

Mikhail Gladkikh,
101000 Moscow
Full color literary almanac. Published annually. 80 pages. USD 10
p/copy.

PARTNIOR (SHA!)

Mikhail Gladkikh, 101000, Moscow.
Literary almanac published 2 times a year. 80 pages. USD 8 p/copy.

196

SLOVENIA

is a Slovenian lesbian, political, social and cultural non profit
quarterly. Its founder and publisher is the lesbian group ŠKUC-LL.
ŠKUC KEKE(C)
Kersnikova 4, si-1000 Ljubljana, Slovenia
tel: +386-61-1304740   fax: +386-61-329185
www: Keiko Suzuki
Publisher: Lezbièna sekcija ŠKUC - LL.
Editor: Natasa Velikonja   e-mail k4fn0030@kiss.uni-lj.si

SOUTH AFRICA

PO Box 28827, Kensington 2101,South Africa
Regularity of Publication: Monthly
Circulation: 20 000   Audited: No
Phone Number: +27-11-622-2275   Fax Number: +27-11-616-6487
E-mail address: exitnews@iafrica.com
website address: http://www.gaynet.co.za/exit/
Editor: Gavin Hayward
Advertising Manager: Ernest Maluleke
Average length of feature: 500 to 1000 words
Minimum rate paid per word: Negotiated
How do you prefer your stories to be filed? Txt
How do you prefer to be contacted? e-mail
What is the best advice for someone contemplating writing for your publication?
Universality, not a plethora of recent, local American or British or
Canadian or Australian references as these would be inaccessible to
many of our readers.

GAY SA Magazine

P.O. Box 1910 Houghton, 2041South Africa
Phone: 011 783 7638   Fax: 011 783 7642
E-mail: gaysa@iafrica.com
Website: www.gaysouthafrica.org.za/newsdesk/gaysamag
Bimonthly   Editor: Andrei Oberholzer

OUTright

P.O. Box 2431 Cresta 2118
Phone: (011) 476 1580   E-mail: outin@iafrica.com
Website: www.outright.co.za
Bi-monthly
Chief Editor: Bryan Robinson

SPAIN

MENsual

Apdo. 2028 - 08080 Barcelona
Telephone Number: 93 412 53 80
E-mail: correo@mensual.com
Website: http://www.mensual.com/

SWEDEN

Kom Ut

Box 350, S-101 26 Stockholm, Sweden
Regularity of Publication: Monthly
Circulation: 12.000   Audited: Yes
Phone Number: +46 8 736 02 17
Fax Number: +46 8 30 47 30
E-mail address: komut@rfsl.se

198

website address: www3.rfsl.se/homoplaneten
Publisher: RFSL - Riksförbundet för Sexuellt Likaberättigande,
(The Swedish Federation för Lesbian and Gay Rights)
Editor: Greger Eman   +46 8 736 02 17
Advertising Manager: Lars Jonsson   +46 8 736 02 17
Minimum rate paid per word: we´re normally not paying
Minimum rate paid for photos: costs for developing them
How do you prefer your stories to be filed? through e-mail
How do you prefer to be contacted? through e-mail or phone
Special needs of your publication: Coverage of debate inside the gay and
queer community in foreign countries, interviews with, and profiles
of, well-known people.
What is the best advice for someone contemplating writing for your publication? Just
to go ahead with it.

QX

Box 17218, 104 62 Stockholm
Tel: 08 720 30 01 or 08 720 40 01   Fax: 08 720 38 70
E-mail: redaktionen@qx.se   Website: www.qx.se

SWITZERLAND

aK

PO Box 7679, 8023 Zürich, Switzerland
Regularity of Publication: Bimonthly
Circulation: 7000   Audited: No
Phone Number: ++41-1-272 84 40
Fax Number: ++41-1-272 84 40
E-mail address: kontiki@access.ch
website address: www.access.ch/ak/
Publisher: Daniel P. Wiedmer ++41-52-720 24 02
Editor: René Hornung
Advertising Manager: Roberto Fischer
aK is the only magazine for gay men in Switzerland. We cover Swiss
issues as well as international ones, especially with gay culture, per-
sonalities and camp issues.

TAIWAN

G&L Magazine

7F #224 Sec.4, Shung-Shiao East Road Taipei 106 Taiwan
Fax 886 2 8773 6867   E-mail: gnl@gnl.com.tw
Website: www.gnl.com.tw
Monthly

THAILAND

Pink Ink

MBE Surawong #227 173/3 Surawong Road Bangkok 10500
E-mail: pinkink@khsnet.com   Tel.: (02) 661-3150 ext 1515
Editors: Nick Wilde, Jennifer Bliss

TURKEY

KAOS GL

Ali Ozbas, P.K. 53, CEBECI / ANKARA, TURKEY
E-mail: kaosgl@geocities.com or kaosgl@ilga.org or
ali.ozbas@isbank.net
Regularity of Publication: Monthly.
KAOS GL has been published since Sept. 1994 regularly. Now, it is
the only gay and lesbian mag published in Turkey. KAOS GL is a
member of the ILGA.
Phone Number: +90.312.4170119-- Please call only at night
Fax Number: +90.312.3639041
E-mail address: kaosgl@ilga.org
website address: www.geocities.com/WestHollywood/Heights/3050

200

The magazine KAOS GL is published by the KAOS group jointly and there is not a certain job division. All business is carried out by volunteers.
Average length of feature: words: 1-2,000
Minimum rate paid per word: KAOS GL includes articles which are written by volunteers from all around Turkey and no fee is paid for articles.
How do you prefer your stories to be filed? Mixed
How do you prefer to be contacted? Through e-mail
Special needs of your publication: Because we do not have a permanent place to meet and conduct our business, we are having difficulty in working efficiently. For renting an office, we need grants and advertisements. We publish anything on gay/lesbian/bisexual/ transgender issues. They can be on politics, religion, arts and culture and health.
What is the best advice for someone contemplating writing for your publication? He or she should write in clear English, so we can translate the article. Any article on gay issues is welcomed.
NOTE: You can read our issues from the 35th on in our web site. But if you would like to have KAOS GL in your hands, please give us an address to mail KAOS GL.

UKRAINE

Nash Mir ("Our World")

PO Box 62, 348051, Lugansk, Ukraine
ourworld@cci.lg.ua
Editor: Andriy Maymulakhin

UNITED KINGDOM

Attitude

Northern & Shell plc City Harbour London E14 9GL
Tel: 0171 308 5090   Fax: 0171 308 5075
Email: attitude@norshell.co.uk

Monthly
Circulation September, 1998, 55,000
Editor: Paul Hunwick

Axiom News   Axiom Magazine

73 Collier Street, London N1 9BE United Kingdom
Regularity of Publication: Axiom News (fortnightly) Axiom Magazine
(Monthly)
Circulation: News-20,000   Monthly -40,000
Audited: No
Phone Number: +44 (0) 171 833 3399
Fax Number: +44 (0) 171 837 2707
General Manager: Louie Mears (ext. 28)
Editor: Paul Disney (ext. 21)
News and Features Editor: Abbie Walsh (ext. 24)
Arts Editor: Antonio Passolini
Advertising Manager: Richard Holloway (ext. 22)
Art Director/Production: David Holt (ext. 27)
Average length of feature: 1200 words
Minimum rate paid per word: negotiable
Minimum rate paid for photos: negotiable
How do you prefer your stories to be filed? PC/Mac Text
How do you prefer to be contacted? Letter and sample of work
What is the best advice for someone contemplating writing for your publication?
Send in sample of work, we particularly are interested in Gay and
Lesbian issues from America and International, as well as British
perspective stories. Our fortnightly newspaper and magazine
are available in metropolitan cities throughout the UK (London,
Manchester, Birmingham, Brighton, Glasgow, Edinburgh,
Liverpool, etc)

Bi Community News

BM Ribbit, London WC1N 3XX
Regularity of Publication: MONTHLY
Circulation: 250   Audited: No
E-mail address:BCN@BI.ORG.   WEB http://bi.org/~bcn/
Minimum rate paid per word: dont pay.
Minimum rate paid for photos: dont pay

How do you prefer your stories to be filed? any
*How do you prefer to be contacted?*e mail
Special needs of your publication: UK community news /reviews with an international readership, humor.
What is the best advice for someone contemplating writing for your publication? If its bi relevant and concerning the UK, write.

BOYZ

Cedar House 72 Holloway Road London N7 8NZ
Phone: 0171-296 6000   Fax: 0171-296 0026
E-mail: boyz@boyz.co.uk
website: www.boyz.co.uk
Circulation: 55,000   weekly
Editor: David Hudson
Deputy Editor: David Marrinan-Hayes
Advertising: 0171 296 6250

Continuum

Unit 4, 1A Hollybush Place, London E2 9QX, UK
Regularity of Publication :   bi-monthly
Circulation: 4,000   Audited: Yes
Phone Number: +44 (0)171 613 3909
Fax Number: +44 (0)171 613 3312
E-mail address: continu@dircon.co.uk
website address: www.virusmyth.com/aids/continuum/index.html
Editor: Huw Christie 613 3941
Assistant Editor: Alex Russell 613 3909
Advertising Manager: Martin Walker 613 3909
Average length of feature: 2,000 words
Minimum rate paid per word: credit, kudos, no cash
Minimum rate paid for photos: credit, kudos, no cash
How do you prefer your stories to be filed? email attachments in Word 5 or on paper with disk
How do you prefer to be contacted? email or phone or letter
Special needs of your publication: Social, cultural, political and scientific discourses around alternative views of sexuality, aids and health; book reviews; news.
What is the best advice for someone contemplating writing for your publication? Ask

for a free trial copy of the journal.

Cross Talk

The Northern Concord,
P.O. Box 258, Manchester, M60 1LN,
Regularity of Publication: Quarterly
Circulation: 800   Audited: No
E-mail address: JennyB@northernconcord.org.uk
website address: http://www.northernconcord.org.uk
Average length of feature: 5 to 6 A3 pages @ 10 pitch
Minimum rate paid per word: All material is donated free of charge
Minimum rate paid for photos: As above
How do you prefer your stories to be filed? Typed or preferably on disk
How do you prefer to be contacted? via e-mail or post
Special needs of your publication: Cartoons, Humor, Book Reviews,
National news, Celebrity profiles, Transgender information.
What is the best advice for someone contemplating writing for your publication? Do it
with the best motives.

DNA Magazine

DNAPublishing Ltd.,
17A Newman Street, London, W1P 3HD
Tel 0171 631 0944   Fax: 0171 631 0955
E-mail: dna.magazine@virgin.net
Monthly

DIVA Magazine

116-134 Bayham Street London NW1 OBA
Regularity of Publication: Monthly
Circulation: 35,000   Audited: No
Phone Number: +44 (0) 171 482 2576
Fax Number: +44 (0) 171 284 0329
E-mail address: diva@gaytimes.co.uk
website address: www.gaytimes.co

General Manager: Chris Graham Bell

Editor: Gillian Rodgerson
News Editor: Vicky Powell
Advertising Manager   Maggie Travers
Average length of feature: 1200-1700 words
Minimum rate paid per word: 10p
Minimum rate paid for photos £25
How do you prefer your stories to be filed? e-mail with hard copy
How do you prefer to be contacted? post or e-mail
Special needs of your publication: Any material to do with lesbian culture, politics
What is the best advice for someone contemplating writing for your publication?
Send SAE if you want mss returned; pitch ideas before writing; we never publish unsolicited poetry

Gay & Lesbian Humanist

34 Spring Lane, Kenilworth, Warwickshire,CV8 2HB,
Regularity of Publication: quarterly
Circulation:1,000   Audited: No
Phone Number: 01926 858450   Fax Number: 01926 858450
E-mail address: GALHA@bigfoot.com
website address: http:visitweb.com/ptt
Publisher: The Pink Triangle Trust 01926 858450
Editor: George Broadhead 01926 858450
Advertising Manager: Roy Saich 01926 858450
Average length of feature: 2,000 words
How do you prefer your stories to be filed? by e-mail
How do you prefer to be contacted? by e-mail
Special needs of your publication: cartoons, humour, national and international news of gay/lesbian/atheist interest, lesbian views.
What is the best advice for someone contemplating writing for your publication?
Become a born-again atheist

Gay Times

Millivres Ltd
Ground Floor 116-134 Bayham Street London NW1
Phone: 0171 482 3571   Fax: 0171 284 0329
E-mail: edit@gaytimes.co.uk   Website: www.gaytimes.co.uk
Monthly

Homosex

Chronos House,
Cedar House, 72 Holloway Road, London, N7 8NZ
Phone: 0171 296 6000   Editor: Peter McGraith.

Metropolis

(formerly "Thud")

VadaVision Limited,
1 Tavistock Chambers, Bloomsbury Way, London, WC1A 2SE
Tel: 0171 831 4666   Fax: 0171 831 4777
Weekly
Email: eng@thud.co.uk

NOW

(North of Watford)

e-mail: editor@nowmag.co.uk
website: www.mowmag.co.uk
Monthly

Pink Paper

Cedar House,
72 Holloway Road London N7 8NZ
Regularity of Publication: Weekly
Circulation: 56,783
Phone: 0171 296 6000   Fax: 0171 957 0046
E-Mail: editorial@pinkpaper.co.uk
Publisher: Chronos Publishing Ltd
Editor: Alistair Pegg   0171 296 6210
News Editor: David Northmore
Sales Executives: Sean Baguley, Ronnie Hunter 0171 296 6110

206

QX Magazine

23 Denmark Street 2nd Floor London WC2H 8NJ
Phone: 0171 379 7887   Fax: 0171 379 7525
E-mail: qxmag@dircon.co.uk
Website: www.qxmag.co.uk
Publishers: Tony Claffey and Ben Schubert (Firststar)
Editor: Tony Claffey

Scene Update

Virtual Universe Ltd.
22 Stephenson Way, London,NW1 2HD
Tel: 0171 388 6689   fax: 0171 388 6649
Circulation: over 30,000   Biweekly

ScotsGay Magazine

PO Box 666 Edinburgh EH7 5YW Scotland
Regularity of Publication: Monthly
Circulation: 5,000   Audited: No
Phone Number: +44 131-539 0666
Fax Number: +44 131-539 2999
E-mail address: editorial@scotsgay.co.uk
website address: http://www.scotsgay.co.uk/
Advertising Manager: Heather - +44 131-558 1279
Average length of feature: 1,500 words
Minimum rate paid per word: Not paid - this is a not for profit publication
Minimum rate paid for photos: Not paid - this is a not for profit publication
How do you prefer your stories to be filed? **Legibly!**
How do you prefer to be contacted? **E-mail**
Special needs of your publication: **Anything of interest to lgbt readers
in Scotland.**
What is the best advice for someone contemplating writing for your publication?
Think Scottish!

Shout!

PO Box YR46, Leeds LS9 6XG
Regularity of Publication: monthly
Circulation: 7,000   Audited: No
Phone Number: 0113 248 5700   Fax Number: 0113 295 6097
E-mail address: editor@shoutmag.demon.co.uk
website address: http://www.shoutmag.demon.co.uk
Publisher and Managing Editor: Mark Michalowski on 0113 248 5700
Average length of feature: 500-1500 (exceptionally) words
Minimum rate paid per word: negotiable per article
Minimum rate paid for photos: n/a - we take our own
How do you prefer your stories to be filed? electronically - emailed ideally
How do you prefer to be contacted? whatever's convenient
Special needs of your publication that freelance writers might be able to fulfill: generally local events, reviews, happenings, politics for Yorkshire and the north
What is the best advice for someone contemplating writing for your publication?
Give me a phone call and have a chat!

HIV/AIDS

a&u America's AIDS Magazine

25 Monroe Street, Suite 205, Albany NY 12210-2743
Regularity of Publication: Monthly
Circulation: 205,000
Phone Number(s):   518 426 9010   800 841 8707
Fax Number: 518 436 5354
E-mail address: mailbox@aumag.org   inbox@aumag.org
website address: www.aumag.org
Please give both the name and the telephone extension or
direct line:
Publisher and Editor-In-Chief: David Waggoner
Managing Editor: Dale Reynolds 323 848 9098
Features Editor: Nick Steele
Arts Editor: Bill Jacobson
Advertising manager: Harold H. Burdick   518 229 8096
Average length of feature: 2,500 words
Minimum rate paid per word: 15 cents per word
Minimum rate paid for photos: $75 or more
How do you prefer your stories to be filed? Mail, fax, e-mail
How do you prefer to be contacted? phone
Special needs of your publication: Materials sensitive to HIV/AIDS
What is the best possible advice for someone contemplating writing for your publication? Read the magazine. Articles in A&U often match the quality found in top consumer magazines like Rolling Stone and The New Yorker.

HIV Plus

110 Greene Street, Suite 600, New York, New York, 10012
Regularity of Publication: quarterly
Circulation: 200,000   Audited: Yes
Phone Number: 212 625 0897   Fax Number: 212 334-9227
E-mail address: hivplusacd@aol.com
website address: aidsinfonyc.org/hivplus

Publisher: Amy Simmons   212 334 9119 (ext. 26)
Editor: Anne-christine d'Adesky 625 0897
Arts Editor: James Condrad
Advertising Manager: Amy Simmons

Average length of feature: 2,000 words
Minimum rate paid per word: negotiable
Minimum rate paid for photos: negotiable
How do you prefer your stories to be filed? on mac disc
How do you prefer to be contacted? phone or email
Special needs of your publication: National news, coverage of racial minori-
ty issues, Lesbian news and views; infectious disease news with an
emphasis on HIV/AIDS

Pink Ink

c/o IAA P.O. Box 71248 Fairbanks, Alaska 99707
Regularity of Publication: Monthly
Circulation: 300   Audited: No
Phone Number: (907) 452-4222 or (907) 455-7055
E-mail address: pink-ink@geocities.com
website address: www.geocities.com/~pinkink/
Publisher: Interior Aids Association (907)452-4222
Editors: Jenn Wagaman (907)455-7055
                Pete Pinney (907)474-1136
                Dena Ivey
                Chris Carpentino
Advertising Manager: Julia McCarthy
Average length of feature: 800 words
How do you prefer your stories to be filed? e-mail
How do you prefer to be contacted? Jenn Wagaman
Special needs of your publication: anything of interest to Interior Alaska
GLBT community. Currently in need of graphics
What is the best advice for someone contemplating writing for your publication? We
are a community project, dedicated to serving the needs of a small
community of people in the Interior of Alaska. We are grant funded,
and cannot pay for submissions, but encourage anyone to submit
news, fiction, non-fiction, poetry, art work.

Positive Living

1313 N. Vine Street L.A. CA 90028
Phone: 323 993 1362   Fax: 323 993 1592
E-mail: PSerchia@apla.org
Editor: Paul Serchia

Positively Aware

1258 W. Belmont Chicago, Illinois 60657-3292
Regularity of Publication: Every two months
Circulation: 100,000   Audited: No
Phone Number: (773) 404-8726 Fax Number: (773) 404-1040
E-mail address:tpanet@aol.com   website address:www.tpan.com
Publisher: Test Positive Aware Network
Editor: Steve Whitson, Ph.D.
Advertising Manager: Jeff Berry
Average length of feature: 2,500 words
Minimum rate paid per word: 40 cents
Minimum rate paid for photos: $50
How do you prefer your stories to be filed? Fax
How do you prefer to be contacted? Phone

Positives For Positives

1714 1/2 Capitol Ave.Cheyenne, WY 82001
Regularity of Publication: Quarterly
Circulation: 4,500   Audited: No
Phone Number(s):   307-635-0566 or 800-492-2203
Fax Number: 307-635-4332
E-mail address: pos4pos@wyoming.com
Publisher: 307-635-0566 or 800-492-2203
Editor: Ditto
Average length of feature: 1,000 words
Minimum rate paid per word: 0.05 cents
How do you prefer your stories to be filed? e-mail in WordPerfect or snailmail
How do you prefer to be contacted? phone
Special needs of your publication: Newsletter is HIV specific, so anything relating to HIV topics.

What is the best advice for someone contemplating writing for your publication? If you can donate work that's great, because I don't always have money to pay. We're non-profit, all volunteer and recieve no government funding. Call before submission if you cannot donate, we'll let you know what the cash flow looks like.

POSITIVE NATION

250 Kennington Lane, London SE11 5RD, UK.
Regularity of Publication: Monthly
Circulation: 22,000   Audited: No
Phone Number: + 44 20 75 64 21 21
Fax Number: + 44 20 75 64 21 28
E-mail address: editor@positivenation.co.uk
website address: positivenation.co.uk
Publisher: Iain Webster
    (publisher@positivenation.co.uk)
Editor: Graham McKerrow
    (editor@positivenation.co.uk)
Managing Editor: Gus Cairns
Arts Editor: Rose de Freitas
News Editor: Roger Goode
Advertising Manager: Craig Adams
    (sales@positivenation.co.uk)
Average length of feature: 900 to 1500 words
Minimum rate paid per word: £50 per feature
Minimum rate paid for photos: £60
How do you prefer your stories to be filed? email
How do you prefer to be contacted? phone/email
Special needs of your publication: Any subject if there is an HIV angle.
Particularly seeking cartoons, humour, celebrity profiles.
What is the best advice for someone contemplating writing for your publication?
Originality, clarity, accuracy, brevity. Positive Nation is aimed at all positive people not just one community, one sex or one racial group.

Positive Times

Cedar House
72 Holloway Road London N7 8NZ
Phone Number: 0171 296 6000   Fax Number: 0171-296 0026

Executive Editor: David Bridle
Advertising Manager: Mike Ross 0171 296 6113

POZ

349 West 12th Street, NY, NY 10014
or
Box 1279 Old Chelsea Station New York NY 10113-1279
Regularity of Publication: monthly
Circulation: 150,000   Audited: No
Phone Number: 212-242-2163   Fax Number: 212-675-8505
E-mail: pozmag@aol.com
website address: www.poz.com
Publisher: Megan Whiting
Editor: Walter Armstrong
Managing Editor: Jennifer Hsu
Features Editor: Esther Kaplan
Arts Editor: Esther Kaplan
News Editor: Ronnilyn Pustil
Average length of feature: 2500 words
Minimum rate paid per word: negotiable
Minimum rate paid for photos: $50
How do you prefer your stories to be filed? fax or email
How do you prefer to be contacted? email or phone
Special needs of your publication: Humor
What is the best advice for someone contemplating writing for your publication? Send
resume and clips to deputy editor Jeff Hoover at the above address.

INDEX

224

Photo by: Russell Maynor

About The Editor

Paul Harris

Paul Harris is freelance journalist and playwright based in New York City and Fort Lauderdale, Florida. He has been published in news-papers and magazines all over the United States including The Advocate, Alternative Family Magazine, A&U, Au Courant, Baltimore Alternative, Bay Area Reporter, Bay Windows, Between the Lines, Blacklines, Dallas Voice, Etcetera, The 4 Front, Fountain, Frontiers, Gayly Oklahoman, Gay People's Chronicle, The Gazette, Genre, Harvard Gay and Lesbian Review, In Newsweekly, Just Out, Letter From Camp Rehoboth, LGNY, Lifetimes2, Metro Weekly, New York Blade, Out, Out 'N About, Out Front Colorado, Outlines, Outword, Philadelphia Gay News, Planet Q, Positives For Positives, POZ, San Francisco Bay Times, Seattle Gay Times, Stage Directions, TWN, Texas Triangle, This Week In Texas, Update, Washington Blade, Watermark, and Windy City Times.

He is the author of four plays that have either been published or produced - "Keats", "To Have And To Hold", "Lost And Found" and "Breakfast With Maria."

A Note From the Editor About the Next Edition

Long before this book went to the printers it was obvious that it filled an enormous need amongst writers, photographers, editors, publishers and activists. It therefore seems highly likely that there will be future editions of the Queer Press Guide. If your publication is listed in the current edition but any of the details about it change in terms of personnel, the regularity with which you publish please contact me at QPGY2K@aol.com or alternatively by sending a fax to 212 265 6845.

On the other hand if your publication is not listed please contact me at QPGY2K@aol.com or by fax at 212 265 6845 and I shall gladly forward you a form to complete so that you will be in the next edition.

Many Thanks,

Paul Harris